NATALIA KULISHENKO

AN ENGLISH QUEEN AND STALINGRAD

THE STORY OF ELIZABETH ANGELA MARGUERITE BOWES-LYON (1900–2002)

ИНСТИТУТ ПЕРЕВОДА

AD VERBUM

Published with the support of
the Institute for Literary Translation, Russia

AN ENGLISH QUEEN AND STALINGRAD

THE STORY OF ELIZABETH ANGELA MARGUERITE BOWES-LYON (1900–2002)

by Natalia Kulishenko

Translated from the Russian by Christopher Culver

Proofreading by Emma Lockley

Published with the support of the Institute for Literary Translation, Russia

Publishers Maxim Hodak & Max Mendor

© 2020, Natalia Kulishenko

© 2020, Glagoslav Publications

www.glagoslav.com

ISBN: 978-1-912894-60-4

A catalogue record for this book is available from the British Library. This book is in copyright. No part of this publication may be reproduced, stored in a retrieval system or transmitted in any form or by any means without the prior permission in writing of the publisher, nor be otherwise circulated in any form of binding or cover other than that in which it is published without a similar condition, including this condition, being imposed on the subsequent purchaser.

NATALIA KULISHENKO

AN ENGLISH QUEEN AND STALINGRAD

THE STORY OF ELIZABETH ANGELA MARGUERITE BOWES-LYON (1900–2002)

Translated from the Russian by Christopher Culver

AD VERBUM

Published with the support of
the Institute for Literary Translation, Russia

GLAGOSLAV PUBLICATIONS

Contents

FOREWORD BY ALEXANDER KRAMARENKO 7
FOREWORD: THE QUEEN MOTHER (TRACES OF A PORTRAIT) 9
PREFACE: TRACING THE FACTS 13
ACKNOWLEDGEMENTS 15
PROLOGUE 16
THE PRINCE AND CINDERELLA (1900–1936) 21
    CINDERELLA'S BIRTH 22
    THE FAMILY TREE OF GEORGE VI 28
    CROWNED COUSINS: GEORGE V AND NICHOLAS II 33
    THE YOUTH OF GEORGE VI 35
    ELIZABETH'S FIRST LOVE 37
    THE FUTURE KING MEETS THE QUEEN OF HIS HEART 40
    FROM CINDERELLA TO DUCHESS 47
    THE DUKE AND DUCHESS OF YORK 50
    AWAITING CHILDREN 53
    THE YOUNG DUCHESS'S STATION WITHIN THE ROYAL FAMILY . . 54
    MOTHERHOOD 57
BECOMING QUEEN (1936–1939) 61
    THE FATEFUL LOVE OF EDWARD VIII 62
    THE KING'S FAVOURITE 66
    A CONSPIRACY AGAINST AN UNSUITABLE KING? 70
    EX-KING, NOW DUKE OF WINDSOR 75
    A KGB SPY IN THE QUEEN'S CHAMBERS 80
    THE ACCESSION OF GEORGE VI 83
    THE CORONATION OF GEORGE VI AND ELIZABETH 85
    TOURING AS A WAY OF BOOSTING
    THE MONARCHS' POPULARITY 88
WORLD WAR II (1939–1945) 93
    BRITAIN'S SECRET WEAPON 94
    ELIZABETH'S INFLUENCE
    AS PRESIDENT OF THE BRITISH RED CROSS 100
    CLEMENTINE CHURCHILL IN STALINGRAD (APRIL 1945) 102

A BRIEF EXCURSUS INTO THE HISTORY
OF THE CITY ON THE VOLGA 107
THE MAN STALINGRAD WAS NAMED AFTER 110
THROUGH THE PRISM OF
AN HONORARY SWORD OF KING GEORGE VI 115
OPERATION MOONLIGHT SONATA AND COVENTRY 124
DUELLING SNIPERS DURING THE BATTLE OF STALINGRAD 130

HER MAJESTY QUEEN ELIZABETH
THE QUEEN MOTHER (FROM 1952) 135
   GEORGE VI EXITS .136
   ELIZABETH II 141
   PHILIP, PRINCESS ELIZABETH'S CHOSEN 145
   PRINCE CHARLES – THE DIRECT
   HEIR TO THE BRITISH CROWN 149
   A LOVE TRIANGLE: CHARLES, DIANA AND CAMILLA 151

THE ROYALS LEAVE THEIR TRACE IN RUSSIA (1990–2002) 157
   PRINCESS ANNE VISITS VOLGOGRAD (1990) 158
   GROUND LAID FOR A VISIT FROM THE QUEEN:
   HER MAJESTY IN RUSSIA (1994) 162
   A SOVIET MEMORIAL FROM
   VOLGOGRAD ERECTED IN LONDON (1999) 166
   AN ENGLISH QUEEN AND STALINGRAD 170
   13 KENSINGTON PALACE GARDENS 176
   A CONVERSATION WITH AMBASSADOR YURY FOKIN 179
   HONORARY CITIZENSHIP OF
   VOLGOGRAD FOR A BRITISH QUEEN 185
   THE MONARCHESS'S LAST JOURNEY, AS SHE WISHED IT 190
   HER FAMOUS BRITISH HUMOUR 194

EPILOGUE:
THE BATTLE FOR THE MONARCHY (TWENTY-FIRST CENTURY) . . . 196
APPENDIX: ELIZABETH ANGELA MARGARET BOWES-LYON
(A BIOGRAPHICAL SKETCH) 201
BIBLIOGRAPHY 203
PHOTOS AND DOCUMENTS 207

Foreword
by Alexander Kramarenko

There could hardly be a better time to reissue Natalia Kulishenko's book *An English Queen and Stalingrad* than now, when the seventy-fifth anniversary of the Battle of Stalingrad is being observed. I know that analogous events are being held in Coventry. But the main import perhaps lies in the fact that during those years when Britain and Russia jointly fought against fascism, the best of our people's national characters shone forth. These are largely features that we have in common, such as a readiness to bear any hardships and fight for our freedom, to rely mainly on our own efforts, to appreciate the simple joys of life and sincere relationships among human beings. Perhaps it comes as no surprise, inasmuch as Britain and Russia, situated at opposite ends of the European continent, bear a special responsibility for Europe's fate, which is convincingly shown by our alliances during World War I and World War II.

All of these qualities were most clearly revealed during the Arctic convoys which delivered arms, matériel, and rations to the Red Army through the ports of Murmansk and Arkhangelsk. Over three thousand British veterans of the convoys, some of whom were a mere sixteen or seventeen years old at the time, are alive today and still look back on those marine operations which were unprecedented in the severity and dangers involved. Unfortunately, only fairly recently and in connection with the end of the Cold War were these men's services justly recognized by their own government. In March 2015 Vladimir Putin, with the consent of his British counterparts, issued a decree that these men would be awarded the Ushakov Medal. As shown by a number of ceremonies carried out by the Russian embassy across the UK, in which official British representatives and veterans' families participated; no political disputes or ideological prejudices can efface the memory of the hardships and sacrifices we suffered together for the sake of saving Europe. Veterans' clasping hands, their reminiscences, and the gratitude of several generations of family members left no doubt that life itself has sifted out all that was superficial or insignificant, leaving in people's hearts that which is most central: true brotherhood. Perhaps that is the true significance of the trials which the people of the Soviet Union and Great Britain endured during the war years, and, as we all know, they were proven worthy.

One brilliant page of this brotherhood-in-arms, which will forever remain among the highest spiritual values of our countries' relationship, was written by the consort of King George VI and then Queen Mother, who throughout her long life enjoyed nothing but love and popularity among the British people. This is the tale that the present book has to tell.

A. M. Kramarenko
Ambassador Extraordinary
and Plenipotentiary

Foreword:
The Queen Mother
(traces of a portrait)

During my time as Russian ambassador (1997–2000) in London, I personally met the Queen Mother on several occasions, and I also witnessed her from the side-lines.

Let me say straightaway that, with few exceptions, the Queen Mother enjoyed perennial esteem among British society, and some of her work was admirable indeed.

The British people remember well how during the war the Queen Mother refused to leave her country, she declined all official recommendations and unofficial exhortations that she seek shelter in Canada. The British people were inspired by the Queen Mother's decision to visit, after the German bombings of London, the places which had seen destruction. This represented a considerable amount of moral support for Londoners. She gave a great deal of attention to the British military, and by the end of her life she held honorary positions in over twenty military divisions in the United Kingdom and Commonwealth countries.

Allow me to mention just one or two aspects of the Queen Mother's work for society that I witnessed.

Firstly, during World War II the Queen Mother focused greatly on the treatment of wounded British soldiers and their comfort (for example, she had a facility built at her ancestral Glamis Castle where the wounded could recuperate), then during peacetime and until the end of her life she dealt with the problems British veterans faced, she took part in veterans' organizations, and assisted in resolving matters that might have seemed personal but which were important for veterans. When our embassy was ordered to award anniversary medals marking the victory in World War II to a large group of British veterans, we were challenged by the official position in which the British are not permitted to accept foreign decorations, the Queen Mother, in tandem with the leadership of the largest organizations who brought together veterans of the Arctic convoys, fought for an exception to this rule and she personally blessed the veterans' participation in the ceremony at our embassy, which was a matter of great satisfaction to the veterans and their families. The Queen Mother agreed to take part, together with the Russian ambassador, in the veterans' events held in St Paul's Cathedral. Moreover, she asked that her gratitude be conveyed to Moscow for this "noble gesture" made to the war veterans. Matters of military burials within the royal family are traditionally the province of the Duke of Kent, who has visited the graves of British servicemen buried in Normandy and other sites in Europe, but the Queen Mother, judging from some of her remarks, was aware of these matters and received "reports" from the Duke following his inspections of British cemeteries.

Work of this kind lent weight to the authority of the Queen Mother and the royal family as a whole, and to a notable degree it softened society's reaction to the various scandals which the younger royals were sometimes involved in.

Secondly, when the decision was made to place at the Imperial War Museum, London, a memorial to the twenty-seven million Russians who perished in World War II – primarily through funds raised by British veterans – the Queen Mother gave her support to this undertaking, which also saw the participation, on the British side, of the Duke of Kent and Secretary of State for Defence, George Robertson. It must be noted that official consent had to be obtained to set aside a portion of land for this monument in this prestigious location. In connection with this need, the Russian embassy asked the Queen Mother for her consent to present her with the *Queen* statuette made by the creator of the monument, a native of Volgograd.

The Queen Mother thanked him and complimented the artist's talent. In separate remarks, the Queen Mother readily supported my comment that the unveiling of this site was also of great importance for Russian citizens, who got an opportunity to bow their heads before the memorial to the Russians who perished in the war and to place wreaths and flowers there. I should note that, according to the Russian embassy, this memorial has never lacked flowers and for Russians it has become a place of pilgrimage during visits to London.

I was greatly impressed that the Queen Mother's venerable age (at the time she was already ninety-nine years old) did not stop her from looking magnificent in a dress that demonstrated her outstanding taste, as well as her usual elegant broad-brimmed hat. She insisted on accompanying the ambassador on the way out of the castle, and she paid no mind to my firm entreaties (for I knew that the Queen Mother had had operations on both of her legs) that she not do that. Later, Queen Elizabeth II, during a summer reception on the Buckingham Palace grounds, mentioned what an impression this Russian gift had made on the Queen Mother, moreover as one made in Stalingrad itself. Clearly it was no accident that the Queen Mother responded favourably when the Volgograd authorities wished to award her the title of honorary citizen in recognition of her actions "arranging aid from the people of Great Britain to Stalingrad during World War II and developing friendly ties with Russia".

Thirdly, the Queen Mother contributed significantly to the work of the National Trusts of England, Scotland and Wales, national charities for environmental conservation and the development of an integral landscape policy across the country. I should note that the creation in Russia of an analogous non-governmental organization – the National Centre for Heritage Trusteeship – drew on the experience of the UK national trusts, as well as a number of other organizations in such countries as Norway, Germany and Japan, with the goal of protecting the environment and natural and historical sites.

Of course, the Queen Mother did not delve into the details of the decisions made in this context, but her name and the image of a monarch concerned with ecological problems, played a significant role in the UK National Trusts' success in their efforts. Moreover, these British organizations – with the help of the Queen Mother – gained the proud legal status of trusts, including matters connected with property, as well as in ensuring the whole nation's access to ecological sites. Also of great interest is the UK's experience in creating economic infrastructure, that is, visitors' centres and shops whose income could be used for making these efforts even better, thanks to the growing numbers of tourists. The Queen Mother, by all accounts, was not only interested in protecting the natural landscape and the historical and cultural heritage of the British Isles, but she also found time to visit various such centres, which had an impact both on bodies tasked with environmental affairs and on ordinary people in the UK.

One might claim that each year the Queen Mother's birthday, especially during her one-hundredth-year jubilee in 2000, took on the quality of a national holiday. Until the very end of her life, the Queen Mother remained at the centre of UK society, she was well informed about life in the country and the problems that it faced, and she did a considerable amount to maintain the monarchy as an essential part of the UK's state structure.

Yury Fokin
Ambassador of Russia
to the United Kingdom
(1997–2000)

Preface: Tracing the Facts

On 12 April 2000, the world's leading television networks announced that Queen Elizabeth the Queen Mother of the United Kingdom had been awarded the title of Honorary Citizen of Volgograd in gratitude for the aid which she and the British people gave to Stalingrad during World War II. This matter intrigued me greatly and for me it marked the beginning of an English queen's Stalingrad story. This book was, from the beginning, written not only for a Russian readership but for a British one as well.

If we look back in history, we see that during the most severe trials, Russia and the UK were always on the same side of the barricades: both in World War I, and World War II.

The main difference in this Russian biography of the Queen Mother, compared to its many analogues written in English, is that this Stalingrad story of the English queen touches on the ties between members of the UK royal family and Russia during World War II, as well as in our own time. Especial attention is paid to the period of the Battle of Stalingrad and the unique affinity between the cities of Volgograd and Coventry. Both the political and personal sides of this English queen's life are examined.

History teaches us to draw lessons, and biographies of extraordinary individuals – through the examples of their lives – help us to get our bearings and find the path to a worthy goal. They teach us to take the initiative, act more effectively and, in spite of all obstacles and disappointments, forge on ahead.

The tensions in global politics in recent years are alarming. Through joint efforts that actively promote harmony, we can achieve a synergistic effort and contribute to a firmer peace.

I hope that this book, as a little piece of history, will be translated into English and serve as an additional impetus to developing ties of partnership between Russia and the UK.

Finally, I would like to invite you, dear readers, to visit the city on the Volga, in order to walk the sacred ground of Stalingrad and see with your own eyes one of Russia's marvels: the monument *The Motherland Calls*.

Thank you for your interest in what I present herein.

Sincerely,
Natalia Kulishenko
Moscow, February 2018

Acknowledgements

I would like to thank everyone who supported me during the research for this book, especially Yury Fokin, Russian ambassador to the United Kingdom in the period 1997–2000, for his invaluable guidance during my work; Her Royal Highness Princess Anne, who gave me her portrait; Jack Harrison, the Lord Mayor of Coventry, for providing me with some important materials; Mrs Elsie and Mr Shaun Kearney, my friends from the UK, for their gift of a valuable English book about Her Majesty during my research; the Battle of Stalingrad Museum and its erstwhile director Boris Usik; and many other people. I am grateful to you all! I must also acknowledge that the publisher Mezhdunarodnye Otnoshenyia has been highly esteemed in my family since my childhood. In my younger days when I would read Mezhdunarodnye Otnosheniya's books in my father's enormous library (for example, *Charles Maurice de Talleyrand*) I never imagined that a time would come when a book of mine, too, found a place among the other volumes of this beloved publisher!

Prologue

Studying the life of an English queen might seem like the task of British authors. And indeed British authors have written about her. In Queen Mother Elizabeth's own country, dozens of books have been written about her. Even my modest collection of books in English contains several tomes about this monarch. In Russian however, books that are personally about her are lacking so far, she is mentioned only in the background in stories of other members of the royal family. Yet even the innumerable British biographies about the Queen Mother show a significant lacuna. With the exception of a few words in one British reference on the Queen Mother, they all fail to explore that part of Elizabeth's life that links her to the city once known as Stalingrad. It is this gap that I, as someone from Volgograd, wish to fill in with my Russian study of the monarchess' life.

Nevertheless, this book covers the period from this long-lived woman's birth all the way to 2002 when she (like in a fairy tale) passed away in her sleep at the age of one hundred and one, attended by her caring daughter Elizabeth II. In that same year I began to gather, study and translate materials and documents that shed light on this monarchess' life.

The Russian ambassador to the UK in the 1930s and early war years, Ivan Maisky, has claimed that everyone to a greater or lesser degree is a reflection of their era. The more interesting that era and the more enterprising the person, the more valuable the study of his or her life is. Elizabeth's life encompassed both world wars, the changing of several monarchs on the British throne, personal drama, and even a breach of the rules of royal succession.

Her life was also unusual in that, due to her non-royal background, she was originally not meant to wear the British crown. But from her earliest years she dreamed of the rule and authority which royalty could bring, and in 1936 her childhood dream came true when she ascended to the British throne with her husband George VI.

Sometimes people who are not initiated into the subtleties of the British court, mistakenly refer to the Queen Mother as Elizabeth I, assuming that if the present queen (her daughter) is Elizabeth II, then that must mean that the Queen Mother was Elizabeth I. In fact, she was simply Elizabeth. The name with a number was borne by another English queen, who reigned from 1558 to 1603. (Do you remember from school the defeat of the supposedly unbeatable Spanish Armada? She ruled Britain at precisely that time.) It was that queen who we count as Elizabeth I.

Why is Queen Mother Elizabeth not considered Elizabeth I, or given any number at all? It is because Her Majesty did not inherit the throne, but rather she became the spouse of the British king. This status is known in Britain as Queen Consort. Yet one might have assumed that not even this lofty title would be given to her, the daughter of a Scottish earl.

Since the seventeenth century, brides for English kings have been sought among the princesses of neighbouring states, often Germany. It was considered unseemly for heirs to the British throne to intermix with their subjects, the representatives of the local English aristocracy. The aristocracy itself was loathe to bow in reverence to those of a similar background. Thus, in order to make their authority firmer, royal families only married those of equal origin.

Long ago, in 1772, King George II issued a decree that children of the royal dynasty could only marry with the consent of the monarch. A later decree of his established that marriages could only be concluded with people of royal blood. However, this did not stop one of the heirs from breaking the age-old tradition in 1923, by taking as his wife Elizabeth, the daughter of a lord. How could such a thing happen?

Let us go back several years.

Late 1999, Clarence House, the Queen Mother's official residence

"Your Majesty, we have received correspondence from Russia," the Queen Mother's private secretary tells her. "The Volgograd authorities ask that you permit them to award you the title of Honorary Citizen of Volgograd."

"Is this their gift for my upcoming one-hundred-birthday?" the honoured lady asks with her natural joviality.

"Your Majesty, this is a token of their gratitude for the assistance which you provided to the city during the Second World War. But journalists will probably present it indeed as a gesture in honour of Your Majesty's birthday."

"Don't they know that it is impolite to point a lady's age out?" The Queen Mother smiles. She has traditionally been kindly disposed to journalists, and journalists in turn adored her. "Let the whole world know, then, that I shall be one hundred years old."

The Queen Mother stares defiantly at her reflection in the mirror above the fireplace and fixes a curl of grey hair that has gone astray from her hairdo.

"Your Majesty looks magnificent at one hundred."

Elizabeth was well aware of this even without her secretary pointing it out. After all, was it not already clear from the entire floor of Clarence House dedicated entirely to her elegant attire? Dresses, hats – no, hundreds of dresses and hats were amassed there. Her collection of inimitable clothes, selected by a designer with a sense for her individual style in lemon, light blue, lilac and other gentle shades, grew constantly and proved an embarrassment for the queen's accountants. Due to the elderly lady's fondness for dresses and horses her cost overruns according to the UK civil list amounted to one to two million pounds sterling, but what could one say to the most beloved woman in Britain?

"Alastair, leave the letter on the table. I shall read it later and decide whether it would be fitting for me to become an honorary citizen of Volgograd."

"The Hero City of Volgograd, as the letter calls it, Your Majesty," her secretary notes.

Oh, yes, Volgograd is heroic indeed!

Private secretary to a monarch is one of the most important positions in the court hierarchy. The private secretary is tasked with – to name only some of their sphere of influence – the royal's schedule of visits and audiences, keeping the royal fully informed about all important matters, organizing royal meetings, and overseeing the archives and the chancellery. George V had said about his own private secretary, "Stamfordham taught me to be king."

The secretary left and the Queen Mother sunk into reminiscences. What else could she do, when the story of Cinderella was so long ago now, when, as if by the wave of a magic wand, she – the daughter of a Scottish aristocrat – had become queen? When her husband the king had left this world half a century ago. When she had outlived all of her old friends and foes.

The inquiry from Volgograd about awarding the Queen Mother honorary citizenship came as no surprise to her. Yury Fokin, the Russian ambassador to the United Kingdom, had already broached this subject with his characteristic diplomacy. The matter had begun to be discussed after a Soviet memorial, the work of Volgograd sculptor Sergei Shcherbakov, had been placed on a London square. This was something her subjects had wished, to pay their tribute to the twenty-seven million citizens of the former USSR who had perished in World War II. She had acquiesced to the will of the British people and assisted in erecting this Soviet memorial by removing various obstacles at the highest levels. Elizabeth sighed. Her memory brought back pictures yellowed by time and her mind journeyed a whole century into the past. Her gaze fell on her childhood portrait that hung to the right of the fireplace. It is actually with the mystery shrouding her birth that the story of her extraordinary life begins.

The Prince and Cinderella

(1900–1936)

Cinderella's birth

On 4 August 1900, the Bowes-Lyon family welcomed its ninth child, a girl. Her father Claude Bowes-Lyon, presumably due to being distracted, registered the birth of his new daughter with some delay, and for this he paid a fine of seven shillings and sixpence. Moreover, he misrepresented the real place of birth and instead of London he put down St Paul's Walden Bury, Hertfordshire, something which, decades later, would confound historians, biographers and journalists who researched Elizabeth's life. According to the laws of that time, since 1861 misrepresenting the date and place of a child's birth could lead to lengthy imprisonment with hard labour. The father however did not even suspect that he was registering the birth of a future queen.

The newborn girl was given the name Elizabeth Angela Marguerite. The people of Britain love long names, each of which means something. Thus, the child was named Elizabeth, for example, in honour of the queen who reigned in the time of Shakespeare. The Bard had mentioned her families abode Glamis Castle in his play *Macbeth*; it was there that he set the murder of Duncan. "Angela" was chosen by her father, for the girl struck him as a little angel. Finally, "Marguerite" was proposed by her mother due to the latter's fondness for the marguerite daisy.

If we look to Elizabeth's family tree, her roots go back to Robert the Bruce, an ancient king of the Scots. In this way, she even turns out to have been related to George Washington.

The family had previously born the surname Lyon, and indeed the image of the lion corresponded to their fearless spirit. However, in 1767 the 9th Lord of Strathmore, John Lyon, made a dynastic marriage with Mary Eleanor Bowes, a lady from a wealthy aristocratic family that had no male descendant to carry the name on. The bride's father asked that John add to his surname Lyon also the name Bowes, and he sweetened the deal with a generous dowry. Thus, two renowned families were joined, and from that time forth its members bore the surname Bowes-Lyon.

Glamis Castle is considered to be one of the most ancient buildings in Great Britain. In ages past its lords had their own armies and even their own executioner, to which the Bowes-Lyon coat-of-arms testifies: two lions rampant and archers' bows. Since ancient times a room, one completely white and bare of furniture, had been kept that was known as the "Executioner's Abode". It is claimed that the castle is haunted by certain ghosts: the Grey Lady, the Vampire Servant, and the phantoms of family foes that had been immured in its walls. Was it from this that Elizabeth drew one of her innate traits, namely to not forget or forgive insult? The infamous Wallis Simpson, she who failed to become queen, would see this quality first-hand.

Elizabeth's father, who became the 14th Earl of Strathmore upon the death of his father in 1904, was not especially wealthy by the standards of that time. Since his father had spent a portion of the family fortune on building Episcopal churches across Scotland, he was forced on several occasions to cover debts by selling off some of his enormous property holdings. In spite of his lofty title, the Earl led quite a modest life, and visitors to Glamis Castle who had never seen the Earl before sometimes mistook him for a farmer and even offered him a shot of whisky.

The heart and soul of the family was the Countess, Cecilia Bowes-Lyon *née* Cavendish-Bentinck. As the daughter of a clergyman, she devoted especial attention to her children's Christian upbringing. Both her own children and the servants adored Cecilia, who called her astute, wise and kind hearted. She had great musical talent. She held the view, typical of that time, that for girls – who would eventually become wives and mothers – it was much more important to have a knowledge of art and culture than the hard sciences. The Countess never had to resort to harsh measures when bringing up her children, for her disapproval calmly expressed was already enough to make her children heed her.

In bringing up her children, she emphasized the formation of a firm character and the shrugging off of any despondency or weakness. Elizabeth excelled in this regard, and all the way to the age of one hundred and one she maintained a cheery mood and did not have to think too much about her health.

Cecilia had her own ideas about how to bring up children. For example, she believed that children should be surrounded by fine things, as this would influence their aesthetic development. She had landscapes hung on the walls of the nursery, and the interior was decorated with the finest furniture. Cecilia believed that this would help her children become better, more generous and happier. In time, this would bear fruit.

Unusually for that time and social class, Cecilia wished to avoid using wet nurses and she breast-fed her own children. Until the age of eighteen months her babies slept in her bed and not with a nanny as was customary. Thanks to this closeness established between mother and baby girl, her daughter always maintained a sense of security and sympathy for the world around her.

Although Cecilia's health worsened significantly after she lost one of her sons in the war, she lived to an advanced age. A grieving Elizabeth, who was then queen, wrote to a friend after her mother's death:

> I have been dreading this moment ever since I was a little child and now that it has come, one can hardly believe it. She was a true "Rock of Defence" for us, her children, & Thank God, her influence and wonderful example will remain with us all our lives. She had a good perspective of life – everything was given its true importance. She had a young spirit, great courage and unending sympathy whenever or wherever it was needed, & such a heavenly sense of humour. We all used to laugh together and have such fun.[1]

Such was the remarkable character of the woman who had the greatest impact on Elizabeth's own personality.

Elizabeth's elder sister Violetta had died in childhood (long before Elizabeth was born) from diphtheria. Another sister, Mary, was already seventeen years old when Elizabeth came into the world. After Mary, the next youngest was Patrick, who would eventually become the 15th Earl of Strathmore. Then followed John, Alexander, Fergus, Rose and Michael. Elizabeth was not the last child, however. When she was about a year and a half old, her brother and playmate, David, was born.

Here one must mention the tragic death in 1991 of one of Elizabeth's elder brothers, Alexander.

Let us return to Elizabeth. When she was a month old, a woman named Clara Cooper was hired as a nanny or governess for her. Clara was the daughter of a tenant farmer (everyone called her "Alla" and years later Elizabeth, convinced of her devotion, would task this woman with caring for her own daughters). According to Alla's account, Elizabeth was a lively and outgoing child, she began to crawl early, she took

---

1   Sarah Bradford, *Elizabeth: A Biography of Britain's Queen* (New York: Farar, Straus and Giroux, 1996), p. 77.

her first steps at thirteen months, and she also began to speak at a very young age. Nevertheless, the small children could be fidgety, and the countess had to calm them down.

Elizabeth and David, as children of about the same age, were fast friends. If this brother had not come along, then the little girl would probably have felt quite lonely in the family castle due to the large gap in age between her and her older brothers and sisters. They would hardly be interested in joining her in the games that she and David, both raised in an environment that was not too strict, were able to play.

One of their favourite pastimes was defending the castle from imagined invaders. They knew a tried and tested way of doing this: hot oil had to be poured onto the heads of those assailing the castle. Instead of hot oil, they used cold water. Visitors to their home were in for a shock as the icy water came down on them.

At the age of five or six, Elizabeth and David would often be truant from their morning lessons. However, they would hide in the attic, where they had discovered a secret store of apples and chocolate. They could spend as much time there as they wished, for the wooden stairs leading up were so rotted that they could not support the weight of adults. Thus, the children were able to escape the pursuit of their tutors.

Yet in spite of such mischief, Elizabeth received a fine education at home. By the age of seven she already had a good knowledge of the Bible and the history of Britain, she could write and write well, and she played the piano. By ten years old, the girl was fluent in French. After Elizabeth had already become part of the royal family, she always looked fondly back on her childhood.

Each of the Bowes-Lyon family's residences was meant to be used during a particular season of the year. Usually the family resided in Hertfordshire, where Elizabeth grew up. In late summer or early autumn they would head for Glamis Castle. For social events and sessions of Parliament the family stayed in London at their luxurious home on St James's Square.

The future royal couple first met when Elizabeth was around five years old and the future king was ten. They met at a children's party. Unlike the outgoing and mischievous Elizabeth, Albert looked very sad. She felt sorry for him and offered him the cherries from her cake.

Though the daughter of a Scottish aristocrat had no chance of becoming queen, even as a girl Elizabeth seemed to be acting out the role destined for her in life, she loved to pretend she was queen. When asked what her name was, she would modestly reply, "I call myself the Princess

Elizabeth." Her childhood idyll came to an end when David, her brother and constant playmate, was sent to a boarding school at the age of ten. This separation hit both of them hard. Elizabeth missed her brother greatly and sought consolation in writing to him.

It was during this period that an attempt was made to send Elizabeth to a school in London. Though she received a commendation for her knowledge of literature, she could never get used to the strict discipline. Her family decided to take her out of the school and have her continue her education at home. It was only natural that a child used to a free life in the countryside in a loving atmosphere, would prefer staying in a family environment over the stiff regimen of a school.

Elizabeth learned of the outbreak of World War I on her fourteenth birthday, 4 August 1914, when she and her mother were in a London theatre. Suddenly they heard the crowd outside in the street enthusiastically shouting. This was how the English greeted the beginning of hostilities. Her elder brothers Patrick, John, Fergus and Michael were sent off to the front and Glamis Castle was temporarily turned into a hospital.

Due to her youth Elizabeth could not work as a nurse, but she readily provided what help she could to the wounded, some fifteen hundred of which stayed at the castle. Soldiers thought of her as better than any medicine. These wounded men arrived at the castle crippled from the horrors of war, but Elizabeth's cheerfulness, generosity and energy had an encouraging effect on these recuperating soldiers. She would sew for them, take down letters to their families under dictation, sing with them, show off her tricks on a bicycle, make recordings of the young soldiers' voices and take photos and send them to their families.

Witnessing the sufferings of others in this way had a considerable influence on Elizabeth's character, it provided a counterweight to her innate carefree and cheery disposition, and it taught her compassion, which would come in handy in the future after she became part of the royal family. For bearers of the British crown over the last century, philanthropy and charity have become their main duties. The institution of the monarchy in the UK has been preserved only because of the good that royals have done for their subjects.

The war brought sorrows for the Bowes-Lyon family personally. In the Battle of Loos in 1915, one of Elizabeth's elder brothers, Fergus, was killed. Then the news came that another brother, Michael, had also been killed. However, because Michael's body had not been found, hope flickered in the family that he had somehow survived. Their hopes were not in vain, three months later they received word that Michael had been taken prisoner and was being held in an enemy hospital with a head wound.

In the aftermath of Fergus's death, the health of their mother began to suffer. Elizabeth's elder sisters Mary and Rose were married and David was away at Eton. The young Elizabeth had to take on ever greater responsibilities. The young lady showed herself to be especially responsible and savvy during a fire at the castle which erupted on a dark December night. While many of the adults around her panicked, she showed that she was capable of dealing with extreme situations on her own. This trait would come in handy on multiple occasions in her adult life at the royal court after she married Albert, the future King George VI.

Amazingly, the UK was rocked by a rumour that Elizabeth was not of aristocratic origin, and it was suggested – without any foundation – that Cecilia was not in fact Elizabeth's real mother. Personally, as a researcher I do not find the arguments adduced to hold water. Let me only add that it suffices to look at a photograph of the Countess of Strathmore, Elizabeth's mother, in order to be convinced, as they look so alike.

The family tree of George VI

Albert, Elizabeth's husband, is better known as King George VI. When he was a child, as biographers note, he was not intended for the role of king, because he had an elder brother, Edward (known as David within the domestic circle). According to the rules of succession, Edward should have inherited the throne.

At the time of these brothers' birth (Edward and Albert were born a year apart), Britain was ruled by their great-grandmother, Queen Victoria. After her, in 1901, the crown went to their grandfather Edward VII, who was known as "Edward the Peacemaker" for his skill in assuaging conflicts between states. Then in 1910, in accordance with the rules, their father George V ascended to power. George V had previously held the title of Duke of York and was the previous king's second son. After the untimely death of his elder brother, George became direct heir to the throne and he also wed Mary of Teck, who had been engaged to his late brother.

From the age of ten, the future Duke of York (and ultimately King George V) was constantly at sea as a naval cadet. He and his sickly older brother were inseparable. The Duke's tutor, John Neale Dalton, insisted that they serve together, for the heir to the throne and the future Duke of Clarence was a frail and apathetic boy, and he only livened up when George was around. Thus, George felt a sense of his own leadership already in childhood when he had to care for his weak elder brother.

Like all naval cadets, George got up at five o'clock in the morning and had to care for his own clothes and shoes. Life at sea taught George order and discipline. Therefore, after he became king, he was always concerned with order in the country and ensuring discipline within his own family.

The young George's knowledge of life and the world was not limited to sea journeys. He studied law at university in Heidelberg, and in Lausanne he immersed himself in German and French, though not very successfully. Later on this insufficient knowledge of foreign languages made

George V loath to travel abroad where he might have to demonstrate his linguistic skills or lack thereof.

At the age of twenty-eight George married Mary of Teck, a marriage which British biographers note was out of love. Their mutual affection was preceded by a sad story. Originally Mary (known before her coronation as May) was meant to be the wife of the Duke of Clarence (the heir to the throne). This engagement had been approved by Queen Victoria herself, though May was the result of a morganatic union. In fact, the poor young woman was set out for the lot of an old maid: she had neither pure-blooded royal ancestry, nor wealth nor dazzling beauty. However, Queen Victoria saw her as someone who would keep the monarchy firm (and she did not go wrong!) and blessed May's engagement first with the sickly heir to the throne Edward, and then (after Edward's untimely death from inflammation of the lungs a month before the wedding) with his brother George.

How did Princess May make such a favourable impression on the demanding queen? It is known that the young lady was very well educated for her time, she had a vast knowledge of art, she was fascinated by the history of the British monarchy and she spoke several foreign languages perfectly. Everyone noticed in her a majesty and queenly restraint. Those jealous of May called her a bore, but the new heir to the throne found her attractive and began to cautiously court her.

Here are some lines from a letter he wrote to her during this period: "[…] I hope I shall see you then, we hope one day you will give us a little dinner […]. Goodbye dear 'Miss May' … ever your very loving old cousin, old Georgie."²

The marriage of George and May proved to be a remarkably happy one. In a letter, George expressed his feelings to his wife as follows:

> [W]hen I asked you to marry me, I was very fond of you, but not very much in love with you, but I saw in *you* the person I was capable of loving most deeply, if you only returned that love … I have tried to understand you and to know you, and with the happy result that I know now that I do *love* you darling girl with all my *heart*, and am simply *devoted* to you … *I adore you, sweet May*, I can't say more than that.³

---

2   Kenneth Rose, *King George V* (London: Weidenfeld and Nicolson, 1983), p. 26.
3   Ibid., pp. 33–34.

Here one ought to dwell for a moment on the figure of Mary of Teck, as it was she who later taught Queen Mother Elizabeth to carry out the functions of a queen. Mary was an unusual representative of the crown and truly concerned with the problems of society. In 1904 Mary asked the Prime Minister to look into the deficiencies of the classrooms and the meals provided at state schools.

During World War I Queen Mary tirelessly worked alongside other volunteers in hospitals, she cared for the wounded and sternly ensured that other members of the royal family were making patriotic efforts for the good of Britain.

The Soviet ambassador Ivan Maisky, having met the queen at an official reception in 1932, gave an unflattering account of Queen Mary in his memoirs. According to him, Mary was aloof during this audience and she had an air of coldness. She would not look the ambassador and his wife in the eye but rather stared at some point above their heads, as if demonstrating that she was only there out of respect for the tradition that the wife of an ambassador should be presented before the sovereign after the ambassador had presented his credentials.

Here, however, we should take into account the fact that relations between Soviet Russia and the United Kingdom were turbulent in these years, and perhaps the Queen was unsure of how to behave in front of envoys of the Soviet state. For the sake of fairness, it must be noted that in 1941, when Britain was overcome by pro-Russian sentiments, Queen Mary also expressed her desire to make a charitable contribution to the Aid to Russia Fund. This is evident from the minutes of the Fund's meeting of 21 October 1941 (a copy of which was kindly provided to me by the British Red Cross).

Mary and the King were of similar mind and temperaments. They agreed together to raise their children with strictness, as they sincerely believed that their children should fear their august parents, something which later led to disastrous results. Some say that this is precisely the right way to raise the children of a royal family, that is, with a constant anxiety with regard to their parents. In his childhood Edward VII had shuddered at the mere mention of his mother Queen Victoria. Then his own son, George V, feared his father. Thus, fear of one's parents was passed down from generation to generation, and this led to the children developing complexes and neuroses.

However, some authors have disputed this view of the atmosphere within the royal family. For example, biographer Kenneth

Rose feels that there are no grounds to consider George V and Mary as especially severe parents.

As I studied the letters which George wrote to his children and to the elder heir David among them, I noted a tone of concern. The King, as his father, was worried about his son and heir, and he chided him for not taking better care of himself. Here one senses worry more than severity.

The next son, Albert, was born to George V and Mary on 14 December 1895 in Sandringham. It was not the best start to life, as this was a day of mourning for his great-grandmother Queen Victoria. It was on that day in 1861 that she lost her beloved husband Prince Albert. Her grandson, the future King George V, wrote her a letter in which he lamented that the boy had been born on such a sad day for her. He asked Victoria's permission to name the newborn child after his late forebear, and he expressed his wish that Queen Victoria serve as godmother to her new great-grandson. She indeed accepted this role, after writing in her diary that she took the birth of the child on this formerly sad date as a gift from God and a special sign. Time would justify this premonition, for the coronation of her great-grandson and godson took place exactly one hundred years after her own.

The boy was named Albert Frederick Arthur George. Growing up in the royal family, Albert experienced the pressure and strictness of life at court from his earliest childhood. Young princes were expected to observe the harsh rules of the court, and there was no place for an ordinary, noisy and lively childhood. Children were forbidden from even running, they were only permitted to walk decorously.

Surrounded by all-powerful relatives (his great-grandmother Victoria, his grandfather Edward VII, his father George V and his elder brother Edward VIII, who all reigned during his lifetime), Albert nevertheless was a bashful child with a severe stammer.

According to a member of the household staff, during a family lunch there was an amusing incident when little Albert tried several times to intrude on a conversation between the adults. Then an angry Edward VII, his grandfather, ordered him to stay quiet until the meal was over. Later the old king finally asked what his grandson had wanted to say. The boy replied that he had only wanted to warn his grandfather that there was a caterpillar in his lettuce, but the old man had already eaten it.

Once, when Albert was only a few years old, George V saw his son with his hands shoved into his pockets. The King was indignant.

"Pockets are not meant for one to keep one's hands in!" he reproached the prince and then ordered the boy's governess to sew the pockets shut on all of his clothes. We do not know whether this helped the boy when he was a child, but there exist many photographs of the adult Albert with this hands hidden in his pockets.

CROWNED COUSINS:
GEORGE V AND NICHOLAS II

In speaking, even briefly, about George V, one cannot overlook a dramatic episode in his life, namely his indirect share of the blame in the death of the Romanovs. Tsar Nicholas II was a cousin of George's, and their mothers Maria Feodorovna Empress of Russia and Alexandra Queen Consort of the United Kingdom, were sisters. The two cousins bore a striking resemblance to one another and always maintained warm family relations.

In 1917 Nicholas II was forced to abdicate, and thereafter a serious threat hung over the lives of all the Tsar's family. The Windsors were the Romanovs' closest relatives. On 19 March 1917, Pavel Milyukov, the Minister of Foreign Affairs in Russia's Provisional Government, wrote to London with the suggestion that the ex-Tsar and his family be afforded asylum in England, since the Romanovs' position was becoming more fraught by the day.

In the minutes of a meeting at Downing Street on this matter on 22 March 1917, it is recorded that "it was generally agreed that the proposal that we should receive the Emperor in this country (having come from the Russian Government which we are endeavouring with all our powers to support) could not be refused."[4]

Milyukov's delay in responding to the agreement on the British side proved to be fateful. During this time, the shock that George V had felt at his cousin's misfortunes had passed, and George V began to think about how sheltering an overthrown sovereign in his kingdom might reflect on the British monarchy. The position on his side turned a full one-hundred-and-eighty degrees: the Prime Minister was told that the King felt Spain or the south of France would be a more suitable place for the exiled Romanovs. This was followed by diplomatic correspondence,

---

4   Kenneth Rose, *King George V*, p. 211.

and precious time when the Tsar's family might still be saved was utterly wasted.

Meanwhile, George V took every step to ensure that his government's initial decision to afford the Romanovs shelter be annulled. A British warship was never sent to the Baltic to take the Tsar and his family, and this in fact proved a death sentence for him. In April 1918 Nicholas II, the Empresses and their children were forcibly removed to Yekaterinburg, where they were executed three months later.

When the first rumours of the atrocity committed against the Tsar's family reached London, the Russian church on Welbeck Street arranged a memorial service for the victims. After this memorial tribute to his cousin George V wrote, "We can get no details. It was a foul murder. I was devoted to Nicky, who was the kindest of men and a thorough gentleman: loved his country and people."[5]

This has been, ever since, not only a dark page of history for the Russian monarchy, but a stain on the Windsors' reputation.

With regard to the Tsar's sister, Grand Duchess Xenia, she spent the remainder of her life in Britain, where George V arranged a house and an annual pension for her.

In 1994 when Elizabeth II, the granddaughter of George V, visited Russia, she was shown an exhibit at the Hermitage dedicated to Nicholas II and his family. The Queen spoke of her grief and her family's sad memories of the episode.

---

5   Ibid, p. 216.

The youth of George VI

Like his father, Albert was not intended to sit on the throne, but rather to serve in the navy. In 1909 he entered the Royal Naval College, Osborne, and from there he went on to Dartmouth, from which he graduated in 1912. After service on the training ship *Cumberland*, he was assigned to the *HMS Collingwood* as a midshipman. Photographs from that time capture a young Albert in a naval college cadet's uniform, and later in the uniform of a lieutenant.

Prince Albert was present at the Fleet Review in Spithead in 1914 at the start of World War I. Around that time his military career was periodically interrupted by poor health. On two occasions he was removed from the ship on account of health problems (during his naval service he had to undergo an appendectomy and he suffered a duodenal ulcer and subsequently had it operated on) and for a period he had to serve on shore at the Admiralty. However, the Prince managed to return to sea and take part in the famous Battle of Jutland, during which he stood in A turret on the *HMS Collingwood*. His calm and composure under enemy fire was gratefully noted in an official communique.

In September 1916 Albert was relieved from the naval service due to further health complications. Nevertheless, in 1918 he found sufficient strength to take flying lessons for the Royal Air Force. The Prince became a pilot before the Armistice and served as a squadron commander before leaving active service. Biographers recount an episode when Albert and his elder brother managed to evade the guards that followed them everywhere, get into a plane on the airfield, and take off. The younger, proud of himself, gave his elder brother a tour of the skies, and they drew great satisfaction as police scurried around below and only sighed in relief when the heirs to the throne landed safely.

Albert showed the greatest talent in sports. He attended Cambridge University, where alongside his studies he played tennis, golf, polo, rugby, cricket and baseball, and he practised target shooting and horseback riding. In 1920 the Prince won a local tennis championship playing doubles with Louis Greig. In 1926 he went down in sporting history when he became the first member of the royal family to compete at Wimbledon. Moreover, Albert was a keen fisherman and never wasted an opportunity to pursue this pastime.

In 1920 King George V granted his son Albert the title of Duke of York. On 23 June of the same year the young duke took his seat in the House of Lords. In his official duties he focused on two main lines: industry and the youth. He served as the first president of the Industrial Society, and in this position his responsibilities included inspecting enterprises, studying living standards for workers and improving sanitation and hygiene at the workplace and improving safety. In 1912 he founded a series of summer camps that brought together boys from different social backgrounds: two hundred sons of the aristocracy and the same number of commoners. These boys would spend time together, put on concerts, and before they parted a celebration would be held where the Duke of York himself would be present. The boys would make an enormous bonfire and sing choral songs. The way in which they spent this time was very similar to Russian schoolchildren's stays at summer camps.

Elizabeth's first love

People today who knew the Queen Mother when she was alive remember her already as an elderly, grey-haired lady. But she was not always that way. What was Lady Bowes-Lyon like back in the post-war years (and here I mean after World War I)? It must be noted that Elizabeth was never an ugly duckling. From the very beginning she was a charming, lively child, and she was compared to a fairy-tale princess. Then she grew up into a pretty girl and similarly into a winsome, smiling young lady. Because she had lived in the countryside, the young Elizabeth retained an original style of dressing, one that was rather bold for her generation. She would display the same life-affirming style to the very end of her life, and she never changed it even during the dark war years, when people tried to coax her into wearing black. "There is no black in the rainbow of hope," she countered.

Chestnut hair, a pale and pure face, bright-blue eyes ...

As one of her contemporaries recalled, she had a way of making it seem like the person she was talking with was the sole object of her attention.

One imagines that this is how she looked to James Stuart, whom some English scholars have identified as the future queen's first love. The two became acquainted in London in the last year of the war. They were introduced by Michael, Elizabeth's brother. The two friends, both James and Michael, were on leave.

How did this war hero, decorated from battle, look to the young Elizabeth? According to surviving accounts from those who knew him, women found James Stuart incredibly attractive. It is claimed that he could conquer a woman without the slightest effort. He was the son of the Earl of Moray and was handsome, intelligent and outgoing. The only thing he suffered from was lack of money. But he was young, and the young aristocrat forged a career that easily remedied this lack. In short, James was considered an enviable suitor for any young lady from the local aristocracy. He was also considered a suitable match for the daughter of the Earl of Strathmore.

At first James was considered a welcome visitor to Glamis Castle; he stayed there from time to time. He was a friend of Michael's and often served as a dance partner for Elizabeth. However, there was an obstacle to their relationship developing any further: James was already engaged to another young lady, her name was Evelyn Finlayson.

In September 1919 James was a guest at Glamis Castle for some ten days. On 8 September a ball was held there, at which Elizabeth danced with him more than with others, and this was noticed by those around them. About two months later, Evelyn and James' engagement was called off, though things had for a while been leading up to this. Now the common acquaintances of James and Elizabeth waited to see what this ladies' man would do next. When would James propose to Elizabeth? Some even assumed that Stuart had already asked her to be his wife and she had accepted, but the matter was being kept secret for the meantime. However, the expected engagement was never announced, and events unfolded in a remarkably unexpected way.

After James was demobilized from the army, he headed to Edinburgh in order to study law. In the same year he grew close to Prince Albert.

The two men met in Brussels. The Prince wanted to have a good time, like men of his age, and be free of the scrutiny of the court and the royal family. However, he was a timid and shy man, and his stammer only made these problems worse. His peer James Stuart knew how to organize such outings, and he was just what the Prince was looking for. The new friends would attend small parties, go to restaurants and paint the town red. It was precisely in Belgium, they say, that Albert became a man.

After these wild experiences in Brussels, Prince Albert offered James the position of being his equerry, with a high salary, a residence at Buckingham Palace and all meals provided. As Stuart was modest in funds, he accepted this offer. His new position generally involved organizing entertainments for the Prince.

In Edinburgh in 1920, Elizabeth was first presented to the court. This debutante, in a white dress and a tulle hat with ostrich feathers atop, was put on display to many. According to the tradition of that era, she handed an invitation over through an official functionary. As etiquette required, she loudly stated her name and dropped her calling card into a special basket. Elizabeth walked down the red carpet towards

His Majesty, surrounded by her many relatives, she bowed and then departed. The season was open.

Then followed a succession of balls, luncheons, teas, weekends, parties and equestrian outings. Elizabeth entered British high society with a light step and a radiant smile. She danced, rejoiced at her success and rejected a succession of marriage proposals from some of the most eminent bachelors in the aristocracy. Among her suitors was a Serbian prince, but Elizabeth did not wish to become a Serbian princess.

The wounded soldiers at Glamis Castle gave way to healthy young people – the friends of the Earl and Countess of Strathmore's older sons. After her son Fergus died in the war, the Countess often suffered from ill health. Her older daughters had already married. Therefore, the young Lady Bowes-Lyon often had to play the role of the matron of the house. According to accounts from that era, all of the young guests at the castle were in love with her.

THE FUTURE KING MEETS THE QUEEN OF HIS HEART

Prince Albert called the date of 20 May 1920 the start of his love for Elizabeth. One can assume that the Prince, on his way to a ball at Earl Farquhar's in the company of his equerry, had already heard about the irresistible charm of the youngest daughter of the Earl of Strathmore.

We know that Princess Mary (Albert's sister) sometimes threw informal parties at her home. Among those attending was her friend, the breathtaking Lady Elizabeth. Some people at the time supposed that she got on well with Edward, the Prince of Wales, and they expected an announcement of their engagement. However, these hopes were groundless, as the heir to the throne was at that time in love with a married woman, Freda Dudley Ward. Yet Prince Albert had probably already developed an interest in Elizabeth.

It is worth describing in greater detail the organizer of the ball, Earl Farquhar. He was a friend of the royal family and famous for the magnificent balls which he threw. In this he was peerless. The whole cream of the aristocracy took part in his galas. Horace Farquhar himself possessed untold wealth, had a stately character and he donated huge sums to charity. It is said that Farquhar maintained an even more luxurious lifestyle than the members of the royal family.

And so, the two friends arrived at the ball. One of them, intimidating and self-confident, turned his attentions for several dances in a row to this one partner, which in itself was tantamount to acknowledging his affections. As they waltzed, or perhaps foxtrotted, their faces gave their feelings away: they stared at one another with merry eyes.

The other friend, timid and even bashful, could only watch these events from the sidelines.

"Who was that girl with whom you were dancing?" Prince Albert later asked James at the ball. Indeed, he had heard the name Elizabeth before. By his own account, it was on this very day that the Prince fell in love with her. James Stuart became the man who introduced the Prince to Elizabeth.

Life occasionally creates these sorts of collisions, when two friends fall in love with the same woman. Why? Perhaps there is an unspoken sense of rivalry between the two men. Or perhaps a woman who has affections for one's friend stands out from the crowd and is perceived as more intimate.

Soon after the aforementioned events, Prince Albert was given the title of Duke of York. After which he was made a Member of Parliament.

In August 1920, on the threshold of her family home Glamis Castle, Elizabeth met Prince Albert and James; the latter had arranged this visit. In spite of him being a member of the royal family, the Duke of York could not compete with his equerry in attracting women. His stammer, a nervous facial tic and excessive alcohol consumption were the reasons why Elizabeth long remained indifferent to Albert's attempts to court her.

The Prince loved the warm and laid-back atmosphere that reigned in the Bowes-Lyon family. It was so different from the strict regimen at the court and the uptight people who dwelt there! The centre of this earthly paradise at Glamis was naturally Elizabeth. It was apparently after this visit that Prince Albert took the decision to propose to her. But without the King's consent, there was no question of this happening: in Britain a marriage concluded by the monarch's child without the parent's consent is considered invalid.

There is an amusing song to the effect that kings, in spite of possessing ultimate power over human beings, are incapable of doing one thing: marrying for love. In a sense, this is true. In 1772 a law was passed in which members of the royal family could only marry with the king's permission, and moreover they were only permitted to marry persons of royal blood.

However, after World War I, another king, George V, faced the challenge of marrying off his four sons, and he asked his Privy Council to re-examine the laws on marriage. It was clear that after a war with Germany, it would no longer be acceptable to seek marriages with German princesses. The suggestion of Prime Minister Lloyd George was taken up and in a patriotic spirit it was decided that the younger princes would be permitted to marry representatives of the British aristocracy. However, the direct heir to the throne was still ordered to seek out a bride among the daughters of other monarchs.

Thus, it became possible for Albert to marry the daughter of a Scottish earl. Queen Mary was informed of her son Albert's interest in the young Lady Bowes-Lyon. She made inquiries about her from those whom she trusted and she received extremely favourable responses.

In the spring of 1912, after receiving his parents' consent, the Duke of York made, through an intermediary, a marriage proposal to Elizabeth and received in reply a polite refusal. Who exactly was representing the Prince to the young lady he loved is not known for certain. But some say that it was Prince Albert's elder brother, the future King Edward VIII, who brought the marriage proposal to Lady Bowes-Lyon.

Some authors have explained Elizabeth's refusal as a tactical decision: she feared the responsibilities and constant public attention that members of the royal family attracted. The young Elizabeth made these same conclusions in a private conversation with the Countess of Airlie, a friend of both families.

However, Elizabeth herself did not shy away from becoming queen after Edward VIII abdicated, and she even convinced her husband to accept the crown.

Probably the reason for Elizabeth's reluctance to marry Prince Albert at the time lay elsewhere. The young lady may well have been dreaming of marrying for ... love. Speech defects are no help in awakening romantic feelings. Moreover, the Earl of Moray's son and her first love, James Stuart, was right there. Rumours were also circulating that she was an acceptable candidate for the bride of the heir to the throne himself. Had she not dreamed of that since childhood?

The Prince of Wales was considered at this time to be the most eligible bachelor in Britain. He was a fair, blue-eyed young man and the future king. In fact, King George V and Queen Mary were troubled that Edward was slow to marry. When speaking with his father Edward admitted that he was loath to wed a foreign princess. George V then gave his preliminary consent to his son marrying a decent English girl of the aristocracy, and thus this permission was extended beyond the monarch's younger sons as had been set down in the historic degree of 1917.

Now all the young ladies in the kingdom were dreaming of the eldest prince, so that by marrying him they could become queen. Edward remained indifferent to their charms, however.

At that same time his brother, the Duke of York, was suffering from an unrequited love. He declared that he would marry only Elizabeth and no one else. The lovesick prince found an unexpected ally in the

Countess of Strathmore. In a letter to a friend, she wrote that she loved Albert like a son; she considered Albert deserving of good fortune and she claimed that any woman who became his wife would be happy. With these remarks she confirmed her reputation as an astute woman.

Deep within her heart, the Countess certainly hoped that it would be her own daughter who would become this happy wife. This wise mother began to influence Elizabeth, and she began by criticizing the object of her girlish affections, James. All of his flaws were pointed to: his broken engagement with Evelyn, which testified to his unreliability; his lack of wealth; his failure to show any initiative towards Elizabeth. In short, Stuart was no longer seen as a welcome guest at Glamis Castle and a suitable match for Elizabeth.

In turn, Queen Mary decided to visit Glamis Castle in early September 1921, in order to get a close look at the young lady with whom her son was in love with. The Queen was hosted by Lady Elizabeth herself. The Countess of Strathmore, as usual, cited ill health. The young Elizabeth's charm showed here, too. The forbidding Queen Mary left the castle certain that Lady Bowes-Lyon was the only woman who could make her Albert happy.

When the Queen explained why she took a liking to the girl, she pointed to the deep knowledge of British history which Elizabeth displayed. But clearly history had nothing to do with it, rather it all came down to Elizabeth's own charisma. Those who fell into her orbit felt an irresistible affection for her. Elizabeth's joie de vivre was infectious, and the way she listened closely to those with whom she spoke, warmed their hearts.

The Queen's visit to Glamis Castle did not pass unnoticed. Rumours began to fly that Lady Bowes-Lyon was being considered as a bride for ... the Prince of Wales. Even by this time in the early twentieth century, the press resorted to sensationalism and unverified claims to boost sales.

We have an account by the Duke of Windsor himself (who was Prince of Wales until 1936, and then King Edward VIII). When he was already advanced in years, he admitted that Lady Elizabeth had dreamed of marrying him in her youth. However, he did not go into the details.

What can be said about this? The Duke had many reasons to hold a grudge against Elizabeth. He was convinced that it was partly her doing that his wife, the Duchess of Windsor, was stripped of the privileges of being a member of the royal family. But it is unlikely that the elderly Duke was being untruthful here, for after all, in his younger days, every young lady in the kingdom did collect newspaper clippings about him and dream of becoming his wife. What shame was there in merely having such a longing?

Upon her return from the castle, Queen Mary declared that she would not interfere in Albert's romantic affairs and she would simply let events take their course. Meanwhile, her son was regularly visiting Glamis Castle and felt at home there. The Countess of Strathmore's sympathy for him has already been noted, and Elizabeth's brothers Michael and David became his constant hunting companions.

Nevertheless, in spite of Queen Mary's reluctance to interfere in Albert's love life, the natural course of events was violated. In order to unblock the Prince's path, it was decided that James and Elizabeth should be separated by sending James to Oklahoma to work in the oilfields. This twist was arranged by the three mothers involved: Queen Mary, the Countess of Strathmore and the Countess of Moray.

One can assume that James' mother also considered Lady Bowes-Lyon insufficiently wealthy for her son and she consented to this step being taken. In early 1922 Stuart (equerry to Prince Albert) left the United Kingdom. Elizabeth took this departure bravely and did not display any emotion at it.

Then, in February 1922 the wedding of Princess Mary was held, where Lady Bowes-Lyon was one of the bridesmaids. This was not a joyful event for the bride, however, because the Princess was not marrying for love.

Some time later Albert proposed to Elizabeth a second time. Perhaps things had changed with James out of the way? After witnessing the sad example of Princess Mary's marriage, Elizabeth again turned his proposal down, but she did this in a rather tactical manner, so that the Prince still had a chance to propose to her again.

A great deal of evidence of Prince Albert's love for Elizabeth has been given to us. We have his letters to his mother Queen Mary, where he claimed that the more he saw Lady Bowes-Lyon, the more he loved her. Another confidant in his love life was Lady Airlie, who heard firsthand from him how much this unrequited love pained him. One can only imagine the heartbreak of a man who suffered from a stammer, a nervous tic, a love that was not returned and the constant comparisons with his healthy, universally loved elder brother.

There was a certain trusted individual (was it not his elder brother?) who gave Albert some useful manly advice: propose to Elizabeth not through an intermediary, as he had done in the past, but directly, face to face. Considering the Prince's speech defect, this was not an easy decision to make.

Meanwhile, Elizabeth continued to move around in society. At a party in 1922 her acquaintance Chips Channon pretended to be able to foretell the future through cards and predicted that Lady Bowes-Lyon would one day become queen. Naturally this was merely a joke, and few could have imagined that this would eventually come true. Elizabeth simply laughed. However, Albert was present on this occasion and cringed. After all, the woman he loved could only become queen if she married his elder brother.

There then happened something which, at an initial glance, seems trivial, but which probably played a decisive role in the future of the British royal dynasty. On Friday 5 January 1923, the British press proclaimed Lady Bowes-Lyon the fiancée of the crown prince. A newspaper said that an official announcement would be made later. When this notorious article appeared, Elizabeth had gone to friends in Sussex for the weekend. Her host, Viscount Gage, was hopelessly in love with her, like everyone else. After the guests read the article, they began to tease the young lady and addressed her as one does a queen with "Ma'am" (as if they had a presentiment of the future). It was noted that this time Elizabeth lost her composure and could not hide her upset from those present.

Here is how Chips Channon recalled this episode: "The evening papers have announced her engagement to the Prince of Wales. So we all bowed and bobbed and teased her [...]. She is more gentle, loving and exquisite than any woman alive, but this evening I thought her unhappy and distraite."[6]

Why was Lady Bowes-Lyon so upset at this article which linked her name with that of the most eligible bachelor in Britain? We can assume that Elizabeth, aware that the contents of this article was fictitious, sensed what a position the press were putting her in. She did not want to become a laughingstock after the real state of affairs became clear.

After the Duke of York found out about the article, he was torn. He was still unaware that this awkward press coverage would in fact help make his long-cherished dream come true. Incidentally, the newspaper subsequently published a retraction. But it was too late. The article had already played its role for ill or perhaps for good. A week after the commotion, Albert headed for Walden Bury to see his beloved. After he first asked the Countess of Strathmore's permission to do so, he invited Lady Bowes-Lyon

---

6   William Shawcross, *Queen Elizabeth: The Queen Mother*: The Official Biography (Pan Macmillan, 2009), p. 148.

to take a walk with him in the park, where he gathered his courage and this time directly, albeit haltingly, asked Elizabeth to be his wife.

While the love-stricken Prince and his beloved are walking in the park, let us return to Chips Channon's memoirs of this period. Channon, an observant man, did not glimpse any changes in their relationship preceding their meeting at Walden Bury. Everyone knew that the Duke of York had been hopelessly in love with Lady Bowes-Lyon for some time now, and they had already grown used to her being indifferent to him. So what did Elizabeth answer this time around?

Her reply was unexpected indeed: "Yes." Channon and the others were amazed when, on (Monday!) 15 January 1923 the engagement of the Duke of York and Lady Bowes-Lyon was officially announced. Chips describes it as follows:

> I was so startled and almost fell out of bed when I read the *Court Circular*. He has been the most ardent of wooers and was apparently at St Paul's Walden on Sunday, when he at last proposed to her. He motored at once to Sandringham and the announcement is the result, the royalties allowing her no time to change her mind. He is the luckiest of men, and there's not a man in England today that doesn't envy him. The clubs are in a gloom.

The Queen Mother later said that she did not marry for love, but rather she came to love her husband after the wedding. What then moved Elizabeth to accept a proposal from this man who was, for the moment, still unloved?

As always, in order for something significant to take place, several factors came together. Let us try to untangle this ball: James Stuart's absence, his lack of any initiative with regard to Elizabeth. The fiancée's age: Elizabeth was already nearly twenty-three, her girlfriends had long since married, and she had already left behind her girlish romanticism. The desire to marry purely for love had given way to a desire to marry a man who was respectable, loving and reliable. Finally, there was the pressure from her mother, who was always on Prince Albert's side, there was the coaxing and admonitions of Lady Airlie and also the Prince's insistent courtship. And the catalyst that drew them to make their fateful decision was the newspaper gossip about her engagement to the crown prince, which put her in an awkward position. In accepting this proposal from the King's second son, Elizabeth also washed her reputation clean and escaped any mockery.

From Cinderella to Duchess

Though Elizabeth became the first bride of non-royal blood in three hundred years, both parents – King George V and Queen Mary – were happy at their second son's choice. Compared to the heir to the throne, the Prince of Wales, who preferred the society of married women to that of eligible young ladies, Prince Albert had chosen what they saw as a worthy match. Nevertheless, not all of his august relatives were thrilled at his "unroyal" choice. Among these doubters was the haughty and beautiful Princess Marina, the wife of the Duke of Kent (Albert's younger brother) – she believed that this union was a misstep.

In his diary on 15 January 1923 the King wrote that Albert had informed him of his engagement to Lady Elizabeth Bowes-Lyon. George V expressed his confidence that his son would be happy with her. In her turn Queen Mary wrote that they were content and her son looked radiant. Albert told his parents that he was very happy and claimed that his fiancée felt just as he did.

Nevertheless, before the wedding Elizabeth made one mistake which displeased her future father-in-law. Before the official announcement of the engagement, she dared to … give a newspaper interview. Thanks to journalists, the public learned from the fiancée herself just how happy she was and what her sapphire-studded engagement ring looked like. However, she declined to give a direct answer to the question of whether the Duke of York had proposed to her several times before she ultimately accepted.

It was utterly unprecedented for the fiancée of a member of the royal family to give an interview. When word of this reached George V, he was indignant. "Members of the royal family never give interviews!" he instructed his future daughter-in-law.

How did Elizabeth react to this?

For the rest of her long life she never again gave an interview. Well, almost never. After her eightieth birthday, having long since left behind that stage of her life when as an inexperienced young lady she had breached the etiquette for royals, and now feeling that she was someone who could set the rules herself, the Queen Mother took the unusual step of being interviewed about her horses and her love for gardening. Later, already after her death, the public learned of her conversations with Sir Eric Anderson, a trusted individual and close friend, which were recorded on tape for the eventual publication of the Queen Mother's memoirs. These meetings were held at the Queen Mother's country estate and the transcribed dialogues are held in the Windsor archives. After Elizabeth II appointed the British writer and commentator William Shawcross to be the Queen Mother's official biographer, he based his book on these recordings.

The wedding of the Duke of York and Lady Elizabeth Bowes-Lyon took place on 26 April 1923, when the bride was twenty-two years old and the groom twenty-seven. The wedding was held in Westminster Abbey, the first such ceremony since 1382 when Richard II married Princess Anne.

A crowd gathered hoping to see with their own eyes the wedding of this son of George V, so that they could later compare it with that of the Prince of Wales, the heir to the throne. No one could have imagined that they were actually witnessing the wedding of the future king and queen.

The bride's dress was embroidered with silver and pearls. Elizabeth maintained, in spite of her short stature at five feet and two inches, a stately bearing. A smile, one which later would become quite famous, crept over the corners of her mouth. The bride lay her bouquet at the monument to the Unknown Soldier. She did this in memory of her brother Fergus who had perished in World War I. Hereafter, royal brides followed this example and it became a tradition.

In Russia a similar tradition exists: on her wedding day every bride, even if she has no relatives who died in war, lays flowers on the tomb of the Unknown Soldier.

After the wedding, the newlyweds were presented at Buckingham Palace by a wedding cake that was 2.74 m tall, which they cut. Being familiar with the British take on the wedding cake, I suppose that the two newlyweds cut the first piece together, and each of those present took some and wished the newlyweds happiness and children. One other interesting piece of trivia is the superstition that if one tries some of the cake before the wedding, then the marriage will soon break down. In reality, the longevity of a marriage hardly depends on a premature bite of cake. Rather, going for the cake so early would simply be a sign of impatience, and as everyone knows, impatient people find it difficult to establish harmonious relationships. Judging from how long their love ultimately lasted, Elizabeth and Albert first tasted the cake at the right time.

After breakfast the newlyweds first went to Surrey for their honeymoon, and then to Glamis Castle. The weather in Scotland was chilly and the newly-minted Duchess came down with a cold. She had a strong cough. Later she would refer to this illness as not a particularly romantic time. Elizabeth apparently needed time to get used to her new responsibilities as a wife. We must recall that she did not marry out of a burning love and desire. This unromantic cough gave her a little time to adapt to being married.

The Duke and Duchess of York

In Russia there is a saying that if one is with one's beloved, then even a ramshackle cottage is as good as paradise. Today few probably subscribe to that. Yet in the Duke of York's words, his wife could turn any old environment into a cosy and comfortable one.

From the beginning of their lives together, the Duke and Duchess of York had for their "ramshackle cottage" the enormous White Lodge, a home in an antique style not far from Richmond Park. Unlike residences in Russia, English homes have names just like people do.

For example, when friends from the UK invited me to visit and gave me their address, I asked what "Pine Glade" meant. Elsie proudly replied that this was the name of their house in the countryside. I could tell from her voice that a residence that had its own name, was prized in that country much more than one with simply a house number on a street.

Today, White Lodge houses the Royal Ballet School. In the past this home was very dear to the heart of Queen Mary because it was connected with so many memories: it was here that she got married, her first child – the Prince of Wales – was born here, and her parents passed away here. Now the elderly queen was happy that her family estate would again be of use for members of the royal family.

While the newlyweds were on their honeymoon, Queen Mary chose furnishings for their home according to her own taste. When the couple returned, Elizabeth praised the appearance of her new family nest, but then got down to completely remaking it. In her mind's eye she was looking for the cosy home of her own happy childhood. Elizabeth chose to recreate the atmosphere of her own childhood home in this new residence.

The little duchess (as she was called) started off by replacing the furniture left by her mother-in-law, and bringing in the boxes of valuable wedding gifts. Moreover, she asked her mother to deliver some pieces of furniture from her parent's home. As a result, White Lodge was turned into a real paradise for these two newlyweds.

The King and Queen, who soon paid a visit, were content with what Elizabeth had done with the place. Queen Mary gave no sign of being unhappy with Elizabeth's transformation of the home. Apparently the new interior was to her taste as well.

Nevertheless, the newlyweds did not stay long at their first residence as a married couple. The home's remoteness from London brought a great deal of inconvenience. The Duke and Duchess's social obligations required them to often visit the capital, and the journey there and back took a long time. They therefore began to search for a home that would be more suitable. They temporarily settled into the Strathmores' mansion at 17 Bruton Street. Then, in 1927 their choice fell on a house at 145 Piccadilly Street, not far from Hyde Park. They were not put off by the fact that this home lacked a name. The Duchess again got down to sprucing up their nest.

According to Marion Crawford (governess to two English princesses), this house was not of an especially impressive size or grandeur. It was an ordinary home which would interest any successful married couple. Let readers judge for themselves: the house was equipped with a lift, a drawing room, a dining room, a room for entertaining visitors, an office, a study and several dozen bedrooms. The entrance to the building was guarded by police. The staff included a butler, the butler's assistant, a cook, a housekeeper, two footmen, a dogsbody, three parlourmaids, three scullery maids, a nanny, a dressmaker, a valet, a night watch, a driver, a stableman and a maid of honour. If you find this list absurdly long, do not forget that we are dealing with members of the royal family.

The Duchess's schedule has been described by her British biographers as follows. She got up at seven o'clock. Until eleven o'clock she dealt with her correspondence, with the help of her maid of honour. A large portion of her time was devoted to charity. Elizabeth supported a very large number of organizations. For example, the Duchess was a patron of the YWCA. Also under her patronage was the Society for the Prevention of Cruelty to Children. According to information which I received from the British Red Cross, the Duchess became an elected member of its board in 1924 and changed this status only in 1936, when Elizabeth headed this organization.

The Duke and Duchess's schedule included social and public events: visits to shelters for the homeless and homes for the elderly, charity balls and events at foreign embassies, the unveiling of monuments and the christening of new ships. It was in this period that Elizabeth first displayed her ability to charm the masses and magnificently handle the sometimes dull responsibilities that came with being a royal-family member. The press affectionately called her the "Smiling Duchess". She was the first representative of the royal family who allowed herself to smile in public.

In October 1923 Elizabeth and Albert travelled to Belgrade, and then they visited Northern Ireland. Their first travels abroad are noteworthy in that the Duke of York at that time could already note his wife's skill in showing herself in the most favourable light. Unlike the other members of the royal family, Elizabeth was not afraid to smile at people. The Duchess might be called a pioneer in flashing a radiant queenly smile. Elizabeth's goodwill subsequently brought her universal love and admiration. In a letter to his father at this time, Albert wrote of how she always knew exactly what to do and always had the right words to say to anyone they met.

On 1 December 1924 the Duke and Duchess travelled to Africa, where they spent several months in Kenya, Uganda and Sudan. Here Elizabeth showed herself to be an avid hunter. During a safari she displayed excellent shooting skills. Her hunting trophies included all manner of animals, from small ones to big game. In this regard, I am reminded of another outstanding woman of the twentieth century, namely Jacqueline Kennedy and her perennial love of foxhunting.

The life that the Duchess and her husband lived in the hunting camp was quite a simple one. They got up in the morning at five o'clock and ate a light breakfast. Hunting lasted from ten o'clock in the morning to six o'clock in the evening with a break only for lunch. After they returned to the camp, they took a bath in rudimentary washtubs, ate dinner and at half past nine they went to sleep.

They slept in tents and sometimes they had to fall asleep to the fearsome sound of lions roaring. One night the wind twice flipped the Duchess's tent over. Nevertheless, Albert and Elizabeth were free from the shackles of palace life and in their solitude they felt happy, or …

Awaiting children

Or nearly happy. Already three years had passed since they had got married. Elizabeth was twenty-five years old and Albert thirty. The royal family could not help but feel uneasy at their lack of children. Unlike ordinary couples, they did not need time to find their footing materially speaking or establish a career. Bearing children and maintaining the royal dynasty was their career. But for the time being, they had somehow not managed to conceive a child.

As often happens in these cases, rumours began to circulate that something was wrong with the Duchess and she was unable to have children. Then people pointed to how sickly the King had been, and they assumed that the fault lay with him.

There was a pleasant surprise for British society when Elizabeth became pregnant and on 21 April 1926 gave birth to a daughter (now Queen Elizabeth II). Princess Elizabeth Alexandra Mary came into the world in the Strathmores' London home at 17 Bruton Street. On 21 August 1930 in Glamis Castle they were blessed with the birth of a second daughter, Princess Margaret Rose.

The long-awaited appearance of children gave birth to new rumours that Elizabeth had only been able to conceive through fertility treatments. It is noteworthy that the birth of the elder Elizabeth (the subject of this book) is also wrapped in mystery: where was she born and why did her father delay in registering the birth? This story of a foggy birth was repeated with the junior Elizabeth: was she a test-tube baby? Medical science gives us a clear answer, however, for at that time it was not yet possible to conceive through artificial means.

The young Duchess's station within the royal family

This marriage, after Elizabeth had taken so long to accept Albert's proposal, seemed to bring her happiness. She also came to love her husband. From the very beginning people had seen in her a born caretaker of the family home, and that is precisely how things turned out. According to witnesses of that long-ago time, the Duke and Duchess were inseparable, happy together and full of tenderness towards one another.

Even the Prince of Wales, who was still the heir to the throne, admitted that Elizabeth's arrival into the royal family brought freshness and livened things up.

The diaries of George V are dotted with mentions of Elizabeth's good qualities. The King felt that his middle son had made a fortunate choice for his wife. In letters to his son, George wrote, "The better I know & the more I see of your dear little wife the more charming I think she is & everyone fell in love with her here."

The Duchess quickly took upon herself various functions incumbent on the royal family. Her first official public appearance as a member of the royal family took place on 30 June 1923, when she appeared with the King, Queen Mary and the Duke at an air show put on by the British Air Force. In July the Yorks made an official visit to Liverpool. Shortly before this the elderly Princess Helena, the Duke's aunt, had died, and the many organizations and societies she supported were suddenly bereft of an honorary patron from among the royal family.

After the Duchess had made her successful debut at official events, many of these orphaned associations asked Elizabeth to serve as patroness. Thus, she supported the YWCA and the Society for the Prevention of Cruelty to Children.

As mentioned above, in October 1923 the Duke and Duchess made their first journey abroad to Belgrade, where they served as godparents to the heir to the throne of the Kingdom of Serbs, Croats and Slovenes. Later their godson would become King Peter II of Yugoslavia.

The winter of 1924/25 Elizabeth and Albert spent in Britain's colonies – Kenya, Uganda and Sudan – and from January to June 1927 they made a round-the-world tour through Australia, New Zealand, India, Malta and Gibraltar.

However, there was one circumstance which, perhaps, had kept Elizabeth back from marrying for so long and now, during her quiet family life, would not give her peace. The universally loved Duchess was troubled by her husband's stammer, which was so awkward to listen to. The Duchess took advantage of the great influence that she had on Albert and in 1926 she convinced him to turn to Lionel Logue, an Australian speech therapist who was able to help in the most difficult cases of speech impairment.

When the Duke went to visit him, the doctor saw before him a thin, sad man with a downcast look in his eyes.

Perhaps Albert suffered from melancholy or depression. Indeed, his speech defect caused him great distress, as it got in the way of being able to easily converse with loved ones and smoothly carry out his public duties. He was, among other things, hindered from public speaking.

Albert now began a long course of treatment. The speech therapist taught Albert to breathe correctly and deeply. Thanks to these special breathing exercises, the Duke managed to conquer his stammer. But the main role in his success, one is led to assume, was Elizabeth's patience and moral support. After learning the techniques from the doctor, she tirelessly helped the Duke practice again and again.

Just like in her childhood, Elizabeth was surrounded by the love of her own family and now her husband's. Any of her shortcomings were forgiven, including her chronic tardiness. At the court of George V, punctuality was especially important. The hands of all the clocks were set a half an hour or even an hour ahead. Of all the members of the royal family the King firmly demanded that one arrive for meals on time.

Only Elizabeth dared violate his edict. Once, when she had arrived late for breakfast, she expressed her apology. Albert was very nervous for his wife. He always had a hard time accepting her tardiness, mainly because he feared his father's wrath. After Elizabeth apologized, the entire family turned towards the king and froze, expecting a storm. "You are not late, my dear," the King reassured his beloved daughter-in-law. "I think we must have sat down two minutes too early." On another occasion, the King expressed his affection for Elizabeth as follows: "Ah, but if she weren't late, she would be perfect, and how horrible that would be."

Elizabeth was equally fond of her father-in-law and, unlike the others, she did not fear him one bit. After the death of George V, she wrote, "I miss him dreadfully. Unlike his own children I was never afraid of him, and in all the twelve years of having me as a daughter-in-law he never spoke one unkind or abrupt word to me, and he was always ready to listen and give advice … He was so kind and dependable."

Motherhood

On 21 April 1926 the evening newspapers announced that Her Royal Majesty the Duchess of York had, at 2:40 a.m., given birth and now mother and daughter were doing well.

In fact, the birth was a difficult one. The baby had come feet first and the mother's state was fragile. The future Queen Elizabeth II came into the world with the help of a caesarean operation.

How did the Duchess of York cope with her parenting duties? Even back in her carefree childhood she had within her an abundance of kindness and cheerfulness, and she was always an exemplar of motherly love. But by the customs of that era, the children of royal-family members were cared for not by their august parents but by nannies and governesses. The Duchess entrusted the care of her newborn little princess Elizabeth to her own former nanny, whom she knew to be a reliable and loyal person.

In 1927, when their infant was now eight months old, the Yorks went on a six-month tour at the request of King George V. This distance from her baby made Elizabeth very worried. She found it difficult to leave their home and their car turned back several times.

The main purpose of these travels was to be present for the opening of the Parliament House in Australia's new capital Canberra. The government of this, the greenest continent, had been hoping for a visit from the crown prince to honour such an important event. The Prince of Wales, handsome and elegant, enjoyed enormous popularity across the British Empire. When it was announced that, instead of this darling of the royal family his awkward and bashful brother would be coming, the Australians felt some disappointment.

The House of Commons, which was supposed to approve the cost estimate for the tour, saw some debate and it was not entirely kind-spirited. Members of the Labour Party called it extravagant and reproached the young Duchess for abandoning her child for so long. After George V reviewed the minutes of this debate, he was outraged by the vehemence of their statements and he stood up for his family members. He reminded Parliament of how important it was for the royal family to visit Britain's dominions. An appearance by these royals personally could do more to strengthen Britain's ties with its colonies than anyone else.

Almost immediately upon their arrival, the Duchess's inherent charm, tact and smile won the hearts of the Australians. As a result, their mission – to witness the opening of the new Parliament House – was declared accomplished, and indeed better than the Prince of Wales himself could have done. George V was pleased and once again admired Elizabeth's ability to win people over. The King, in turn, informed her in a letter that at the age of eleven months the baby princess already had four teeth.

When the couple returned home, Princess Elizabeth had grown. Her nanny had taught her to say "mama". However, because her mother had not actually been there personally, the child called everyone around her mama. When her real mother finally arrived, the little girl did not recognize her and gripped her nanny's skirt as if on grabbing onto a lifesaver. The Duchess took little Lilibet (as she was affectionately called) by the hand and led her outside with her onto the balcony as she greeted the nation after her six-month absence.

Elizabeth, having been born into a stately family, unconditionally accepted the rules that reigned within it. She also taught her own daughters that they must acquiesce to the requests of the King and Queen as if they were orders. For example, when the frosty Queen Mary suggested to her grandchildren that they visit a museum or an art gallery, the little girls had no right to refuse, no matter how loath they were to go.

Governess Crawford arrived in Princess Elizabeth's household when the latter was only five years old. Still, the little girl's pastimes had little resembled the jolly and carefree picture of ordinary childhoods. The child had never once got dirty as children are supposed to do. Only once at the age of two was she permitted to make a sand castle. For fun the girl visited the park or played quiet games more appropriate for grown-ups than for children bursting with energy.

Now the new governess taught the little princesses to play hide-and-seek and cowboys and Indians. Crawford had the girls travel in the upper seating of a double-decker bus, showed them the London Underground and took them to drink tea in a cafe for ordinary people.

The schedule was approximately as follows. At half past seven the nanny woke the little princesses up. After breakfast they were taken to see their parents and they spent some fifteen minutes with them.

For the rest of the morning Crawford taught them lessons. At eleven o'clock there was a break similar to that in an ordinary school when the pupils go to have lunch.

During the afternoon the children would walk around outside. When it was rainy outside, the princesses drew instead. Around five o'clock came the traditional British tea time, and after that the Duchess came to get the children and she would play with them or read to them.

After dinner, they spent a few more happy minutes in their mother's company, and then the nanny would say that it was time for bed and take the children to have a bath. Sometimes, if the Yorks were not home, the Prince of Wales stood in for them. According to Crawford's account, the Prince of Wales too read bedtime stories to his nieces. The elder princess always retained good memories of this and her warm relationship with her uncle even after his disgrace.

The princesses' education left much to be desired, but their parents did not seek to burden them too heavily with activities. The important thing, they felt, was that their children should be happy. The girls' grandmother, Queen Mary, thought differently and would point out to her daughter-in-law how the girls' education was deficient. This was virtually the only disagreement between her and the Duchess of York.

The girls did not have friends of the same age. Sometimes they would shyly smile and strike up a conversation with children with whom they wanted to make friends, but this was not encouraged. Consequently, the little princesses' best friends had to be their toys and their pets.

King George V adored his granddaughters. He especially spoiled the older of them, Lilibet, and seemed to already glimpse in her an heir to his throne. To other people the old king could seem stern and severe, but for his beloved granddaughter he would happily get on all fours and let her play horsey. Later George V would say, "I pray to God that my eldest son will never marry and have children, and that nothing will come between Bertie and Lilibet and the throne."

BECOMING QUEEN

(1936–1939)

The fateful love of Edward VIII

I now come to one of the culminating moments in the history of the British monarchy, one which opened a path to the throne for Elizabeth and her husband. This drama of one man, King Edward VIII, played out precisely in the way that some of Britain's senior politicians of that time insisted it should. Edward was short-sighted, gullible, somewhat childish and vulnerable, and he was unable to continue holding onto the throne that his forebears had occupied for a thousand years.

But let us go through the facts of this story in order.

Edward was Albert's elder brother and the crown prince. Before he became king, he was known in his family as David. It has been claimed that the little prince's first nanny was sadistic. Aware that George V had no tolerance for children's crying, she would surreptitiously give the child painful pinches, causing him to cry and thus making his parents upset, upon which the sobbing child and his nanny would be sent away. Later on the nanny's warped behaviour was discovered, but it remains an open question just how much influence she had on Edward's personality and subsequent life.

Thus, the heir was brought up under extreme strictness and he desperately needed maternal attention and affection, but this was precisely, according to the views of his royal parents, what he was not supposed to have. After all, he was the future king and he had to bear matters stoically, he could not be spoiled.

The mentor and role model to the young prince was his grandfather, the charismatic Edward VII. But in 1910 the old king died and George V ascended to the throne. During the coronation of George V in the cathedral, the crown prince had a front-row seat. David was the first to bow his knee before his father who had just been proclaimed king, and he swore to him, "I, Edward, Prince of Wales, do become your liege man of life and limb, and of earthly worship; and faith and truth I will bear unto you, to live and die, against all manner of folks. So help me God."

An entry in the diary of George V about this occasion states: "I nearly broke down when dear David came to do homage to me, as it reminded me so much of when I did the same thing to beloved Papa, he did it so well."

Following this coronation, David was given the honorary title of Prince of Wales. A British monarch has the right to grant this title to any of his sons, but usually it is granted to the direct heir to the throne. The investiture ceremony consists of the father bestowing on the chosen son a ring, a sword and a coronet.

In fact, the relationship between George V and his heir was a rather complicated one. We have an account from 1921 of the Prince of Wales' condolences to his relative Mountbatten as the latter was grieving the death of his father: "I envy you a father whom you could love. If my father had died, we should have felt nothing but *relief*."

Some biographers of the royal family claim that George V (who was Duke of York before his coronation) identified more closely with his second son who bore the same title of Duke of York. He considered the marriage between Prince Albert and Lady Elizabeth to be a successful union and he was very fond of his amiable daughter-in-law. She lived up to his expectations, bore two charming little princesses, dedicated herself fully to charitable endeavours and knew how to win over people. In the eyes of the nation, the Yorks were an ideal model of a happy family. It was obvious that this middle son and his wife would carry on the traditions of their august parents, something which could not be said about the no longer young yet still unmarried Prince of Wales. Many in the kingdom wondered when the heir to the throne would marry, but he did not reveal plans to do so.

It is possible that Edward's bachelorhood was initially decreed by the King, inasmuch as the King forbade him from seeking a bride among the local aristocracy (only the daughters of other monarchs were permissible). To enter into a relationship with a young lady without intending to marry her would be dishonest and could soil the girl's name, and was completely unacceptable. The choice of foreign princesses was not abundant due to certain limitations: the King was not permitted to wed a Catholic and German princesses were no longer popular under the new wave of English patriotism. Moreover, Edward wanted to marry solely for love but none of the royal daughters sparked such feelings in him.

The Prince found American women charming, however. They were more free-spirited and less complicated than the women in his own country. He even declared in a speech during a visit to the New World that he could certainly see himself marrying an American woman. All in all, Edward enjoyed the atmosphere of nightclubs and the society of women with painted nails and free mores.

From his early childhood, the heir to the throne had disliked the strictness and ceremony of the royal court. At official events he showed great modesty, and he responded to the incessant ovations directed to him by saying that he understood that the applause was for the King's son, and not to him personally for any special merits. Nevertheless, he enjoyed an unprecedented level of popularity among his people.

At times when the very institution of the monarchy was in crisis, as could be seen by the fall of the Romanovs in Russia, the Hohenzollerns in Germany, the Hapsburgs in Austro-Hungary and the antimonarchy sentiments within Britain itself, the Prince of Wales could still, with one of his appearances, delight the masses. Everywhere he was met with a warm welcome, adulation and applause. This was not only due to his striking appearance: blue eyes, blond hair and a sad expression. His impressionability betrayed in him a man who was capable of compassion and sympathy. He found it easy to relate not only with lords but with his ordinary subjects.

When the Prince inspected factories or visited homes for the indigent, he would delve into the problems of the poorest classes of society and sought to improve these people's lot. During the miners' strike he contributed his own money to the striking labourers. All of this was unusual and it rather alarmed the ruling elite in Parliament: was the future monarch infringing on their estate? Indeed, according to the British constitution, the king reigns, but he does not rule.

The Prince of Wales' education, which had begun at Osborne as a cadet and continued at the naval college in Dartmouth, was completed at Oxford, where he lived a completely carefree life. Besides acquiring knowledge he played golf, cricket, mastered equestrianism (after all, he would have to review parades on horseback!) and went foxhunting. Most of all, he loved playing football, and an emergency council was even convened once at the palace when a photograph had been taken of the heir to the throne lying on his back on the grass during a game of football. After a lengthy debate on whether such poses were worthy for a member of the royal family, he was nevertheless permitted to adopt them.

Edward's academic success was not especially brilliant, but during this time he did acquire valuable experience of participating in political debates.

Upon the outbreak of World War I, and after stubbornly wrestling with the authorities, the Prince of Wales managed to get permission to go to the Western Front, where he gained respect from the soldiers and officers there. He made a quick visit towards the theatre of operations, but as the heir to the throne he was protected and once an attack began he was removed to a safe place. It was at this time that he turned down the Military Cross, stating that he had done nothing outstanding during the war, but he knew many brave men who truly deserved the decoration who had so far gone unsung.

The King's favourite

The fateful woman who changed the course of the British royal dynasty was an American called Wallis Simpson, *née* Warfield. She was born on 19 June 1896 in Pennsylvania to an eminent yet poor family. After the early death of her father, she and her mother were left destitute. The girl was taken in by a rich relative. She received a respectable education and at school she established useful ties with the scions of the establishment. As she matured, Wallis became a very attractive woman. While she lacked outstanding beauty, men found her irresistible thanks to her wit and her keen sense of dress. As men found Wallis attractive, she sought a good match. She suffered from always being seen as a poor relation, and she felt it important to make a worthy marriage with a respectable and wealthy man in their circle. An eligible man was soon found. He was a naval officer with a brave and dashing appearance, Earl Winfield Spenser Jr. At the age of nineteen Wallis married him. However, her choice was not a good one, for Spenser was pathologically jealous, boorish, alcoholic and sadistic.

When drunk, he would lock his wife in the bathroom for the night, destroy all the furniture or start a fight. Wallis told her trusted kin that she intended to seek a divorce, but her relatives were horrified, for there had never been a divorce among the Warfield's and it was considered a great shame – what would people say? To a degree they were right: a divorced woman would find no acceptance among decent families. Thus, Wallis received no support from her relatives, and her unhappy marriage continued for a little while longer.

Later Spenser's duties sent him to China and Wallis went with him. Here, in the permissive and licentious atmosphere that reigned, he spent his time in dens; not only was he not embarrassed by his wife's presence, but, on the contrary, he sought to drag her down too. Some writers have suggested that it was in China that Wallis mastered the art of seduction before she then used it on influential men.

Be that as it may, the resolute Wallis found within her the strength to put an end to this relationship with her mentally unbalanced husband and she filed for divorce. Soon afterwards she found her next companion. His name was Ernest Aldrich Simpson, born to an American mother and an English father. Simpson was a wealthy man, owner of a shipping company, decent, though himself a divorcee. He was kindhearted, and he had connections among the upper circles of British society. It was in Britain where they decided to make their home.

It seemed that all of Wallis's dreams had finally come true, and she began making a new family life in London. England's capital heartily welcomed the Simpson's and the couple began to be seen at the best homes in the West End. Viscountess Furness, also an American by birth, became a confidante to Wallis. The beautiful viscountess, though married, was at the time having an affair with the most enviable bachelor of the Old World – the Prince of Wales. It was in her house, at a grand reception, that the fateful meeting of the Prince of Wales with Mrs. Simpson took place.

At the time they met in 1930, Wallis looked older than the future king, she was homely, lean, with a boyish figure and an unpleasantly husky voice.

Edward asked Mrs. Simpson if she missed American central heating here in England. Simpson retorted that she was disappointed, for any American lady in England was asked the same question, and she expected something more original from the Prince.

The heir to the throne, who had grown used to universal adulation, was intrigued by this bold American woman. The real drama, however, came only three years later. British society learned about their relationship. Rumours reached the King's ears. He was alarmed by his eldest son's melancholy and the dubious way of life that the heir maintained. George V decided to take a decisive step to break this impasse.

First of all, he allowed the Prince to renovate Fort Belvedere (not far from Windsor) as a countryside residence for the heir. Secondly, he reminded his son that as king, he would not object to his son marrying a girl from a local aristocratic family, as Albert had done with Elizabeth.

This solution might be called a significant turn in the history of the British monarchy, but the heir to the throne did not take advantage of this newly-granted right. He seemed to always walk on the edge and test the limits of what was permitted to him. His relationship with the married Wallis Simpson was meanwhile gaining momentum.

As for Elizabeth, her hostility to her brother-in-law's affair was not something that was typical of her. She had easily found a common language with the Prince of Wales' earlier darling, Lady Furness. But Elizabeth had little love for Wallis Simpson due to the latter's coarse and boorish behaviour, as well as for the fact that Wallis had made fun of the Duchess and her role as a respectable mother to her family. Once, when Elizabeth walked into a room, she discovered Wallis imitating her own gestures and facial expressions to the others present.

Of course, Elizabeth and Wallis were completely different kinds of women, both in terms of their appearance, and in their behaviour and in their status. Elizabeth had, even in these early years, tended to be overweight, while Wallis remained scrawny into her old age. The Duchess of York, surrounded by a loving husband and two charming little girls, enjoyed great esteem within the royal family. She was part of a privileged circle around His Majesty and was already well liked by the British people. When on solemn days she appeared before the nation along with other royal-family members on the Buckingham Palace balcony, she too was loudly applauded. Mrs Simpson on the other hand was, with the burden of her dark past, *persona non grata* for King George V and Queen Mary.

For the time being, however, Elizabeth kept her feelings to herself. After she became queen – indirectly helped by Wallis and instead of Wallis – Her Majesty Elizabeth The Queen Consort then followed through and stripped Edward's unwanted wife of the honours accorded to members of the royal family. But that was only later, and meanwhile …

On 6 May 1935 George V marked his reign's silver jubilee. The Prince of Wales brought Wallis, against his father's will. The King was extremely upset at his son's action, which went well beyond the bounds of propriety, and he could now see how far his son's passion for this married woman had gone. George V did not bother reproaching his son, as it would have been pointless. But before his own death the King predicted that within a year of his death, Edward would be completely discredited as king. George V knew well that authority, even if it was authority one had inherited, required prudence and discipline. The heir's inclination to live it up and indulge his own vices did not suggest that he had the firm hand that a ruler needed.

In the last days of his life the old King sought solace in his grandchildren. One of his favourite pastimes was looking out from Buckingham Palace with binoculars as little Princess Elizabeth waved goodnight to him from her window in her house opposite.

It was at this time that the King, utterly disappointed by his elder son, said, "I pray to God that my eldest son will never marry and have children, and that nothing will come between Bertie and Lilibet and the throne."

On 20 January 1936 King George V passed away. David Prince of Wales was the legal successor and he was proclaimed King Edward VIII.

After Edward became king, he declared Mrs Simpson the official lady of his house. A noisy crowd often gathered at Fort Belvedere. Documents of national importance lay on the royal table for anyone to see, not just Wallis but the rest of the guests too. To ministers' horror, on some documents there was not only the imprint of the royal seal but the bottoms of wine glasses. Soon the King had had enough with all this paperwork, which along with confidential documents began to be sent back not only without the King's signature but never having been opened at all.

Wallis herself had boundless influence over the King. It was observed how she would kick Edward under the table when she wanted him to shut up, and she would freely tear the cigar from his mouth when the monarch was smoking in what she considered an inappropriate place.

Once the two lovers visited the Yorks family home, the Royal Lodge. Mrs Simpson led the King to the window and suggested that some trees be planted to improve (as she saw it) the view. Elizabeth and Prince Albert showed an English restraint and did not say a word in response. After all, this garden was especially dear to them. Albert had personally tended to it and watched it bloom. Nevertheless, some changes were made to its appearance as Mrs Simpson recommended.

Soon the King's affections came to the notice of the press beyond the shores of Albion. The press in the United Kingdom had traditionally been reluctant to tar the reputation of the new king in the eyes of the nation, but the American press had managed to get some photos of the two lovebirds in swimsuits while they were cruising the Mediterranean on their yacht, and they reported this romance sensationally to boost sales, proclaiming on the pages of newspapers that a lady from their own country was the future queen of Britain.

Meanwhile, Wallis had not even divorced her second husband yet. A twice-divorced American woman – this was already more than enough to knock her out of the running for the consort of the man wearing the British crown. The wheels of constitutional crisis began turning frightfully.

A Conspiracy Against an Unsuitable King?

The chronology of these long-ago events ran as follows: Edward expressed his desire to marry Mrs Simpson. As he planned it, on the day of his coronation scheduled for 12 May 1937, he would have to step into Westminster Abbey already a married man, so that the woman he loved could be crowned alongside him on the same day. Edward's intentions caused great consternation among the country's ruling elites and the Church. They saw his aim of setting the British crown on an American, and moreover one who was twice-divorced, as something that would undermine the monarchy's authority in the eyes of the people.

Or was this merely a pretext?

Meanwhile, Wallis was filing for divorce from Mr Simpson so that she would be a free woman in time for the coronation. Prime Minister Stanley Baldwin threatened that he and his cabinet would resign if the King went through with his marriage plans, and then the monarch would have to find another politician capable of heading the new government. In any case, this would cause a constitutional crisis and, consequently, the country would potentially collapse. Edward examined various options for marriage, including a morganatic union in which case their children (should they have any) would not be able to inherit the throne. However, the Prime Minister remained adamant that Edward would have to choose between the monarchy and Wallis.

And so, Baldwin threatened to resign, and the King in turn threatened to abdicate. Ultimately it was the Prime Minister who prevailed in this confrontation. On 16 November 1936 they had a decisive conversation in which Edward declared that he had made his decision to marry Mrs Simpson, even if it cost him the throne. This is probably what the Prime Minister had been hoping to extract from him. Baldwin himself – a contented family man – had shown himself to be cunning in his affairs. For example, Lord Halifax described him as an old fox.

A precedent for abdicating from the throne had already been made by the last Russian Tsar Nicholas II, who was a relative of the British royal family. Edward would have to repeat this dramatic step, though his reason for doing so was of a completely different nature.

On that same evening the King, while he was still king, met with his mother Queen Mary and told her what he had decided. The elderly Queen was deeply hurt. Some biographers claim that she never forgave him for renouncing the throne. Many years later Edward attended Queen Mary's funeral and he wrote to Wallis that his mother had been just as cold a person in life as she now was in death.

The following morning Edward informed his brothers, the Dukes of York, Gloucester and Kent. The princes objected to Edward's refusal of the throne. His immediate successor Albert expressed his worries that he would not be capable of coping with the responsibilities of king. Later, he complained to his private secretary that he felt like a lamb being led to the slaughter. He knew that if he had to rule Britain in the place of his elder brother, then it would be the end to any carefree and anonymous life.

However, this was only his initial, knee-jerk reaction. Several days later the Duke of York told the same secretary that if worst came to worst, he was prepared to do his part and lead the nation. Who helped him make this decision and accept the crown? Was it Elizabeth? According to chronicles, in these anxious days she was laid up with a lung inflammation. Was the Duchess in any state to make such a fateful decision and give advice to her husband?

She probably was. Support for this claim consists in the following. The Yorks were always distinguished by their unanimity, and the leading partner in their dance together was the Duchess. Albert could hardly take such a significant step as accepting the crown without obtaining her agreement first. Elizabeth herself later claimed that she had never sought to become queen, but when the time came, she saw it as her duty.

Confusion reigned in the country. The value of the pound sterling fell. The darling of the nation, King Edward, had abdicated, and it was unclear who would take his place. The law on abdication required that Parliament needed to be involved. It fell to Parliament, together with the departing King, to choose the most suitable successor.

Initially the government was hesitant to accept the Duke of York as a candidate due to his history of poor health and his stammer. They also rejected Prince Henry, a rude and uncultured military man, and they instead proposed that the youngest of the brothers be made king, an energetic thirty-four-year-old, who already had a male heir of his own. But as was eventually discovered, the Duke of Kent was a drug addict (though other sources claim that by this time he had already freed himself from this addiction).

Thus, the choice fell on the Duke of York. Even if Albert's history of ill health put his candidacy in question, everyone expressed their confidence that the Duchess of York was magnificently up to the task of dealing with her duties as Queen Consort.

Over the last thirteen years of her marriage, she had already established a reputation for restraint, the elegance of a true lady and a sense of duty placed above all.

According to Elizabeth's account, when Albert found out that he would be proclaimed king, he spent a great deal of time crying on her shoulder. He loved his elder brother dearly and could not cope with this change. Moreover, the newly-chosen monarch was scared of his new role; usually the parents must prepare the crown prince for such a role from his early childhood. Albert did not feel ready. "If someone called us now, how should I introduce myself?" a bewildered Albert asked his wife on that day.

For over half a century, biographers, historians, psychologists and writers have tried to understand why Edward VIII would refuse the throne in order to marry the woman he loved. Several acute questions arise here. First of all, how was an unglamorous and no longer young American able to so easily win over the king that he would refuse the kingdom for her sake? And secondly, how did Baldwin's threats manage to dissuade the king from taking the throne which was his by right?

Edward himself explained his commitment to Wallis by saying that it was the first time in his life that he had met a woman with whom he could speak about his concerns as an equal. The love-stricken king had a lofty opinion of his paramour's mind. As everyone knows, men see sharp wit in a woman as a sign of intelligence, and Mrs Simpson had this quality in spades.

Perhaps Wallis, as a woman who was self-confident and free of prejudices, was for the King a symbol of his own protest against the shackles of palace life. Perhaps inside he was still the little boy deprived of maternal affection and of his father's approval, brought up instead in the strict and stern atmosphere fated to members of all-powerful royal families.

As far as Edward's defeat in his confrontation with the Prime Minister is concerned, the reason for this remains unclear. As king, he lacked only the right to marry a Catholic, but Wallis was not a Catholic. Nor was he forbidden from marrying a foreigner. As for her divorces, there had already been precedents for a king's choice of bride being a divorcee. Was Edward undermining the institution of the monarchy? His subjects adored the young, modern and charming king and even came out in protest to demand that he be allowed to marry the woman whom he loved.

Apparently, Edward was simply weak. Britain's governing authorities simply took his throne from him and made him believe that he himself had voluntarily abdicated.

It has been claimed that there were political factors involved in Edward's abdication. The King had never hidden his pro-German views. A marriage to Wallis, who had considerable influence over the sovereign, would only exacerbate the problem, as British intelligence was well aware of her special bond with Germany's foreign minister Joachim von Ribbentrop. Thus, pointing to Wallis's previous marriages could serve as an excellent pretext for getting rid of an unsuitable king with a dubious paramour.

How did Wallis react to such a huge step being taken for her sake? The moment when Edward abdicated, his beloved was far away from Britain, and so he was able to think clearly without being under the influence of her charm. Throughout history, lovers have often dissuaded a king from abdicating. Due to the impossibility of becoming Queen Consort, she expressed her agreement with remaining in the role of his favourite. But Edward showed here a great firmness and at the price of the kingdom he married Wallis. Eyewitnesses claim that when Mrs Simpson was informed of the abdication by telephone, she exclaimed "The fool!" and burst into tears.

On 10 December 1936 King Edward VIII signed the act of his abdication. William the Conqueror must have been rolling over in his grave: his descendent had surrendered, without a fight, the kingdom which William had won in bloody fighting nearly a thousand years before!

On 11 December 1936, Queen Mary, gaunt with worry, of both the former and the present king appeared before the microphone to deliver a speech. Her clothing hung on her majestic person. For as long as she lived, Queen Mary, who was in spirit an unbending guardian of the monarchy, never recovered from this reckless act by her firstborn son.

There is no account of how Queen Mary felt about the throne being handed to the senior successor over her head. We do know, however, that she hoped that the illicit passion between Edward and the married Wallis would not last long.

It is worth reproducing here some passages from her radio address in order to convey the emotion of this situation:

> I need not speak to you of the distress which fills a mother's heart when I think that my dear son has deemed it to be his duty to lay down his charge. I know you will ever keep a grateful remembrance of him in your hearts. I commend to you his brother. I ask you to give to him the same full measure of generous loyalty which you gave to my beloved husband.

After Queen Mary, the former king spoke to the nation. All of Britain listened to Edward with bated breath. During this time, a seven-minute pause in telephone communications was recorded, that is, the same amount of time as the King's speech, no one called anyone in London. Such a thing had never happened before in the world.

"I have found it impossible to carry the heavy burden of responsibility and to discharge my duties as king as I would wish to do without the help and support of the woman I love."

The same could have also been said by the new king, his successor. And it would be true. Because Albert could not have borne the weight of his duties as king if it were not for the woman he loved, his wife Elizabeth. He in fact said as much when his turn to address the nation came: "With my wife and helpmeet by my side, I take up the heavy task which lies before me."

These were no empty words. Indeed, for the entire length of his reign (1936–1952) Elizabeth took an extremely active role in ruling the nation. Not a single important matter of state importance was tackled without her being part of the discussion, not a single meeting with the Prime Minister took place without her being consulted first. Not a single document for the King's signature went out without her consent.

Ex-King, now Duke of Windsor

As I will hardly be returning to the matter of King Edward VIII, let me describe what subsequently happened to him. Now holding the new title of the Duke of Windsor he left his native land. On 3 June 1937, he married forty-one-year-old Wallis Simpson in France. All of their royal relatives had been invited to the wedding, but none of them responded to this gesture. His brother, now King George VI, merely sent him the letters patent setting out that neither the Duchess nor their issue had the right to be addressed as "Your Royal Highness". "This is a fine wedding present!" Edward bitterly said about his brother's action.

While Wallis might not have been a great beauty, in this era she was the talk of the town like no one else, overshadowing royals and Hollywood stars. She was criticized, she was admired and imitated, and her name never left the newspapers. But the Duchess of Windsor was refused the honour of being called "Her Highness". Even the vicar who came to the French château to marry the couple was later stripped of his own position. Thus, the monarchy got its revenge on those who dared undermine it.

At first, after Edward's abdication, his brothers would telephone him. More often it fell to the ex-king to show the initiative. On the one hand, he would call his younger brother with the purest of intentions, in order to provide wise counsel on fulfilling the duties of a king. On the other hand, during these conversations Edward would try to extract some privileges for himself. He tried, ultimately unsuccessfully, to have the title of Her Royal Highness extended to Wallis.

But George (or Elizabeth) held firm on this point. It was precisely the impermissibility of allowing "that woman" to become part of the royal family which had been the official reason for Edward's abdication. His act would lose all meaning if she were allowed to style herself Her Royal Highness. Time and time again George said no.

Soon the telephone calls between the two brothers came to an end. And this is how it happened. One evening, George VI was informed that the Duke of Windsor had rung from Austria. The King rang back, but the telephone operator responded that the Duke was in a hurry to get to a dinner party and would call him back when he returned. The King was hurt by this brusque and careless attitude and Elizabeth felt forced to take measures to protect His Majesty from such disrespect. The royals' telephone operator was told that no calls from the Duke of Windsor were to be put through. When this ban on communication with his brother reached Edward's ears, he shrewdly noted that this was not the doing of his soft-skinned brother but of his revengeful wife.

Another appalling story connected with the Duke of Windsor has been set down in the memoirs of Walter Schellenberg, where he tells of German intelligence's 1940 attempt to kidnap the Duke in order to put pressure on the British government. Edward was famous for his pro-German feelings, and Hitler planned to put him back on the British throne in exchange for his loyalty. However, the Windsors departed just in time for the Bahamas, where Edward was fulfilling the role of governor and Wallis was assisting the local Red Cross.

The Soviet ambassador Ivan Maisky, then in London, made a curious mention of this fact in his diary on 17 August 1940:

> The duke of Windsor has arrived with his Mrs Simpson in the Bahamas, where he has been appointed governor. Essentially, of course, this is exile. Why has the former king been treated so harshly?
>
> I've heard from excellent sources that Queen Elizabeth is behind it all. She is "master" of the house and has the king under her thumb. She is awfully jealous. She has set herself the task of bringing popularity and splendour to the royal family. She sends the king everywhere – to camps, factories, the troops, the frontline – so that he should appear everywhere, so that people should see him and grow used to him. She never rests either: bazaars, hospitals, telephone operators, farmers, etc. – she visits them all, gives her blessing, graces with her presence, parades. She even pulled off the following, highly unusual stunt recently. The Queen's brother, who serves in MEC, arranged a private tea party, to which a dozen prominent American journalists were invited. The Queen attended the party, too, and for an hour and a half she "chatted graciously" to the correspondents, together and individually. But not, of course, for the papers. The queen is

terribly afraid that the Duke of Windsor might return home and "steal" his brother's popularity, which required so much effort to achieve. That is why the Duke of Windsor was exiled to the Bahamas.[7]

When the Soviet ambassador made this note (one that is very important for the historical record and also rather sarcastic towards Elizabeth), he did not tell the whole story of how far the former king's sympathies to the Nazi regime went. Now, after new evidence has come to light, one can see in Elizabeth's behaviour a genuine attempt to protect the monarchy from the shadow that the Duke of Windsor's unpatriotic inclinations might cast over it.

What ultimately resulted from Edward's rejection of the kingship for the woman he loved? After he escaped the prison of palace life, he entered another prison, that of Wallis. According to his barber, Edward would leap up and run to heed her call about any trifle, even if it were during a haircut. It was a relationship that was more fitting for a slave than a king.

But his gifts were equal to those of a king's: the Duchess received such a huge number of precious items that people were baffled why the wife of an ex-king should need so much jewellery. All of these gems and pearls were authentic and worth a fortune.

Were Edward's feelings returned? Some biographers refer to a supposed dossier which had been compiled by British intelligence when Wallis was still Mrs Simpson. Allegedly, in this dossier figure the names of her lovers whom she was meeting with at the same time as her romance with Edward. Among them are a playboy, a car dealer, and an infamous political figure, Ribbentrop. The last is said to have even sent Wallis a bouquet of roses, the number of flowers which corresponded to the number of nights they had spent together. Such negative evidence against her made it impossible to consider Wallis a candidate for the role of queen. It was clearly for this reason (and not merely her being twice divorced) that the government was completely opposed to her accession to the throne.

What kind of relationship did Wallis and Edward have now that they were married? Several years after their wedding, the press reported that Wallis was having an affair with a friend of the Windsor family, Jimmy

---

7   Ivan Maisky, *The Maisky Diaries: Red Ambassador to the Court of St James's, 1932–1943*, ed. by Gabriel Gorodetsky (Yale University Press, 2015).

Donahue, a millionaire who was twenty years younger than the Duchess. Their affair was so ardent that the ex-king's wife nearly moved on to a fourth marriage. But this young lover was a volatile type and he even raised his hand against the Duchess. Much later, after their affair had already passed into oblivion, Donahue was found lifeless at his home, his room decked with portraits of Wallis, whom he seemed to have never forgotten. There was something about this woman that could drive men mad.

The Duchess herself, in her memoirs *The Heart Has Its Reasons*, stated that for her the meaning of life in their marriage was making the Duke happy. After he abdicated, she realized how strong his feelings for her were, and ever since then she had constantly felt a responsibility to live up to the high position to which his love had elevated her. The Duchess sought in every way to ensure that their life was the kind that Edward was used to, that is, a royal life. They lived in a luxurious château in France (a residence bought from Charles de Gaulle), and she ensured that the ex-monarch's days were filled with social events so that he would never have time to grow bored.

For as long as they were married, wherever they appeared all eyes would be on them. The Duchess realized that everyone would gawk at the woman for whom a man had given up his kingdom, and so she always dressed in the finest haute couture and shone with countless diamonds. In 1937 she was named "Queen of Elegance", and famous designers like Coco Chanel, Balenciaga, Elsa Schiaparelli, Christian Dior and Givenchy would always send her their latest creations in recognition of her exquisite taste.

The Windsors remained married to the end, and only Edward's death in 1972 parted them. Before he passed away, Queen Elizabeth II came to see him. Before meeting with the Queen, the dying man wanted to stand up in order to greet Her Majesty. The Duke's doctor, amazed at such recklessness, warned him that he might give up the ghost at any moment. Edward nevertheless greeted the monarchess in a way that was fitting for royalty, and not lying down in bed. Under his jacket one could see the line leading from his intravenous drip, which was hidden behind a screen, and the Duke heroically rose to meet his niece as if it were no big deal at all.

Their conversation was kept strictly confidential, but over time some details have become known. The former king said that he did not fear death, but he was worried for his wife. She would be all alone without him, and after they both died they wanted to be buried together in the royal cemetery. Elizabeth II told her uncle not to worry and she promised to carry out his last wish. After this sad meeting had ended and the Queen had left, she was seen to be in tears. Perhaps she had remembered how her uncle had read bedtime stories to her when she was small? Or was she thinking about her first, sole and victimless love for Prince Philip?

She fulfilled the promise made to her uncle and she took it upon herself to pay the Duchess's bills. Though the latter owned countless jewels given to her by her husband, she lacked ready cash to pay for the château's upkeep. Once widowed, Wallis lost interest in life and became reclusive. She remained faithful to the memory of her husband who had given up his kingdom for her sake. The Duchess survived her husband by another fourteen years and died in 1986 at the age of ninety. In her last years she was paralysed and in a vegetative state.

A KGB spy in the Queen's chambers

In connection with the matter of the Duke of Windsor (the ex-King Edward VIII), I must mention one more fact that links the British royal family with Russia. It concerns one of the members of the infamous "Cambridge Five". This man was an advisor to the King, and at the same time a Soviet spy, and his name was Anthony Blunt. Viktor Popov, former Soviet ambassador to the UK, has written in depth and entertainingly about this matter, and I will only briefly mention it in passing.

Anthony Blunt was born into the family of a vicar and his mother was a cousin of Lord Strathmore (Elizabeth's father), and so Blunt was a relation of the Queen. When he came of age, he chose to study art history and became very prominent in this field. In spite of his kinship with royalty, Blunt was not a supporter of the monarchy and his curiosity led him to consider the new socialist system in the Soviet Union. During his studies at Cambridge, Blunt came under the influence of Communist ideology, where art was given a deservedly high place. When the threat of fascism hung over the world, Blunt reached the conclusion that he ought to lend help to the Soviets, and therefore he was already prepared ideologically when Soviet intelligence recruited him. Thus, an English art historian and a relative of the royal family served, for many years (starting from 1937 and including the post-war era), as a Soviet spy. Soviet intelligence highly appreciated his collaboration and his contribution to our victory in World War II. Several times he was offered awards and even a pension after his spying career ended, but each time Blunt firmly refused to accept any money. His efforts for Soviet intelligence were done out of his ideological principles.

Throughout his colourful and risky life, thanks to his hardworking nature and his talent, Blunt held high positions in his native country. During the war he served in MI5 and there he was able to acquire the information needed to battle fascism. Later he was hired at the palace as an adviser to King George VI and subsequently Queen Elizabeth II, a role usually given to only the most trusted people in the monarch's circle.

How did a Soviet agent merit such a venerable place in the palace hierarchy?

In 1945, when the war against Nazi Germany was over, Anthony Blunt was sent there by the monarchy on a secret mission, along with another trusted person, Royal Librarian Owen Morshead. His assignment was a difficult and delicate one: to seize any correspondence between Germany and the British royals which might compromise the latter. Evidence that the Duke of Windsor had met and talked with Hitler would be a black stain on the reputation of the British royal family.

As Ambassador Popov explains in his study, the contents of these documents are not known for sure, but they remain classified at the insistence of the British. But even in 1945 it was not easy for Blunt to get his hands on them.

After the fall of the Third Reich, the documents belonged equally to all victor nations. How could the British reach an agreement with all parties? The King's envoy had to be crafty. At that moment, these materials of so delicate a nature were being guarded by the United States' Women's Army Corps. The female captain obviously refused to simply hand over the documents. Blunt then distracted her with some polite conversation in order to allow the other agent to spirit the materials away. Their outing was a success, and several tons of potentially compromising materials were brought back to Britain.

Thus, Blunt had carried out a mission of the greatest difficulty for the British royals, and so he became one of the King's trusted individuals and was even granted a title.

Decades later, in 1979, Prime Minister Margaret Thatcher told Parliament that the name of one more member of the Soviet spies known as the Cambridge Five had been discovered: it was the art historian and friend of the royals, Professor Anthony Blunt. This revelation stunned everyone. But even more astonishing in this detective story is that British intelligence had for years held evidence of Blunt's espionage, but no measures were taken against this traitor. Why?

Any publicity risked a huge scandal. This failure on the part of British intelligence was too shameful and would harm its reputation. Therefore, MI5 decided to keep quiet about this particular spy, unless the press decided to take the matter up and run with it.

A consequence of the British intelligence's failure was the Soviet spymania in 1971, when the English government deported one hundred and five Soviet diplomatic personnel.

According to the facts set out by Ambassador Popov in his book, the situation changed after a new British embassy was built in Moscow on Smolenskaya Naberezhnaya. When the new building was constructed, the English were particularly concerned about security and protecting themselves against Russian intelligence and counterintelligence. The construction works were carried out solely by British experts, using materials brought from the UK. Imagine the huge cost of such things as special bricks, impenetrable to electromagnetic radiation. All types of communication were filtered, and the building was equipped with the highest protective measures.

From this, as Popov sees it, one can conclude that the British were superior when it came to spying, since unlike the UK embassy in Moscow, the Soviet embassy in London was poorly protected from eavesdropping, which made the goings on at the embassy an open book.

What of Blunt's subsequent fate? Moscow had expected him to eventually be found out, and offered to help him escape the UK. By this time, however, the eminent art historian was no longer so enamoured with the superiority of the communist system and he honestly admitted that he could not live under such circumstances. Whatever the future might hold, he preferred to remain in his native country. When British intelligence exposed Blunt, the two parties reached an agreement that was mutually beneficial. The former KGB agent lived out the rest of his days as a free man in his home country. Only a few people attended his funeral, and many of the wreathes were laid anonymously. Such is the lot of spies. No one came from the Soviet side, perhaps in order to avoid drawing renewed suspicion to Blunt's former contacts.

The Accession of George VI

Albert's ascension to the very top was not easy and it involved all kinds of troubles. At first, many were reluctant to see him become king. The British people, as is well known, do not like change. They had long since grown used to the idea that Edward, with his romantic aura, would be king. Now their beloved Edward had been cast out. The press dug up his unexemplary record at the military academy. What was also mentioned was the new king's speech defect and his weak state of health. The newspapers printed unpleasant comparisons with his elder brother.

During this period, Albert's stammer grew stronger, though he had begun to get rid of it through the breathing exercises with the speech therapist Lionel Logue and with Elizabeth's support. Albert became king in circumstances that were personally harsh and unpropitious for him.

In spite of whatever external factors that might have shaken his self-confidence, the new king behaved from the very beginning like a sage politician. Was it perhaps because he had behind him a woman with a firm and unbending spirit? During these days that were so anxious for Britain's monarchy, Elizabeth wrote to the Archbishop of Canterbury: "I can hardly now believe that we have been called to this tremendous task, and the curious thing is we are not afraid. I feel that God has enabled us to face the situation calmly."

Of all the many names available, Albert chose the most appropriate for this troubled time: George VI. For the nation this name would represent continuity and the carrying on of the tradition of his father George V.

The next pragmatic step he took was in choosing the name for his elder brother. George objected to the proposal that the ex-king should be simply called Edward Windsor, saying that Edward was the son of a duke and had the right to maintain that title. Moreover, in order to prevent his elder brother from engaging in politics, he was allowed, as before, to be addressed as His Royal Highness The Duke of Windsor. Without this title, the ex-king would have been permitted to freely express his opinion on political matters. Still, the ghost of Edward as a figure loved by the public still haunted Buckingham Palace. We have testimonies from this period to the new King's lack of self-confidence and excessive suspicion.

George VI was just as deliberate in the choice of his coronation date. The preparations for a coronation are long and important. Only after the coronation can a king be considered God's anointed. However, these preparations had originally been meant for Edward VIII, and too much expense had gone into them already. The new sovereign decided not to wait the recommended one-year period but instead chose to be crowned on the day meant for Edward. He sent a telegram to Parliament saying that while the king involved would be different, the date would remain the same.

The Coronation of George VI and Elizabeth

After her accession to the throne, Elizabeth became Queen Consort. Usually the role of Queen Consort is a purely ceremonial one of accompanying the king. But it was not Elizabeth's character to play such a passive role, and she began actively helping her husband George VI in every way possible.

The King's gratitude to his wife for her support was expressed on 14 December 1936, on his own birthday (he turned 41). In accordance with the tradition set down by his father, George VI awarded Elizabeth the Order of the Garter. Earlier, King George V had on his birthday bestowed the same order on his wife, Queen Mary.

The Order of the Garter was created in 1348 by King Edward III and it is the highest chivalric honour in Britain. The reason for its founding was a curious incident. As the legend goes, at the ball celebrating the seizing of the French port of Calais in 1347, the garter of one of the ladies – the King's favourite – fell to the floor. The King picked it up and, after he saw the men of his court sniggering, he proclaimed, "*Honi soit qui mal y pense*", that is, "Shame on him who thinks evil of it". These famous words became the Order's motto.

Buckingham Palace is the residence of the British monarchs. According to its inhabitants, it is not exactly the most comfortable place to live in the United Kingdom, but the British monarchs are obliged to reside precisely there. In his time Edward VIII had said that the palace reminded him of a crypt with its endless, gloomy corridors and old-fashioned rooms.

Buckingham Palace was built in 1703 and originally belonged to the Duke of Buckingham. King George III then bought it from the Duke. Only with the reign of Queen Victoria, however, did it become the official residence of the royal family.

The new reigning couple, too, were forced to move to Buckingham Palace and leave their comfortable and homey White Lodge behind. This took place on 15 February 1937. The little princesses – ten-year-old Elizabeth and six-year-old Margaret – reluctantly left their childhood home and were astonished to hear that, alongside all the other changes in their lives, they no longer had surnames. This coming after Margaret had only recently learned to write her former surname York. Soon, however, Buckingham Palace was transformed. In the suites for the royal family's use, Elizabeth managed to create a cosy environment. George VI proudly noted that his wife could turn even the gloomiest place into a real home. Buckingham Palace is too big to ever redo it all, and so these changes concerned only the rooms for the King and his family.

Coronation Day was set for 12 May 1937. Everyone prepared for this august event in their own way. The King devoted himself to his breathing exercises with his speech therapist in order to eradicate his stammer, which had flared up again. He also learned how to wear the crown, which was so heavy that it would result in a headache after wearing it only for a few minutes. The Queen had magnificent coronation dresses sewn for herself and her princesses. Ten people laboured to embroider the emblems of all the parts of the British Empire on the Queen's mantle.

Later, Chips Channon recalled that Elizabeth looked marvellous on this day like never before. Incidentally, Elizabeth was the first British queen since the time of the Tudors to actually be born in Britain.

Chips had been in love with her when she was still a young lady. Now, when Elizabeth had blossomed into a beautiful mature woman, he felt that she had become even more charming. Elizabeth's round figure at the coronation did give rise to rumours that she was pregnant, but these were unfounded.

On that day the King and Queen got up at three o'clock in the morning. The state flags were raised, the red carpet was rolled out for the royal family and the abbey. Foreign monarchs, presidents and prime ministers had arrived beforehand. Something that was unprecedented in the history – centuries long – of crowning British monarchs, was that the ceremony would be broadcast over the radio. Another noteworthy feature was that the widowed Queen Mary was also present, though that was not the custom. It is known that on this day recognizing "God's anointed", Mary handed Elizabeth a small book and told her, "Here you will find everything that a queen needs to know". In other words, how to be queen.

Both of the little princesses admirably withstood the long procedure to crown their parents, which lasted a good three hours and forty minutes. The King and Queen knelt together with the Archbishop. The Archbishop prayed for them and blessed them. When the crowned couple got up from their knees, there were tears in their eyes. This coronation ceremony made a strong impression on the eleven-year-old princess, the future Queen Elizabeth II. She asked her grandmother then, Queen Mary, what the latter remembered of her own coronation, and Elizabeth was astonished at Mary's reply that with time she had already forgotten all about it. Perhaps the august dowager did not want to recall how scared and awkward she felt at her own ceremony.

There is an account of the 1911 coronation by one of her subjects:

The Queen looked pale and strained. You felt she was a great lady, but *not* a Queen. She was almost shrinking as she walked up the aisle giving the impression that she would have liked to have made her way to her seat by some back entrance: the contrast on her "return" – crowned – was magnetic, as if she had undergone some marvellous transformation. Instead of the shy creature for whom one had felt pity, one saw her emerge from the ceremony with a bearing and dignity, and a quiet confidence, signifying that she really felt that she was Queen of this great Empire, and that she derived strength and legitimate pride from the knowledge of it.[8]

But let us now return to the 1937 coronation and one incident connected with it. Due to a mix-up by the abbey personnel, the crown was placed the wrong way around on the head of George VI. Furthermore, one of the bishops accidentally stepped on the long hem of the royal mantle, which nearly caused the king to stumble as he was walking forward.

What are we to make of these inauspicious signs? With many years of hindsight, one might see in them harbingers of World War II that came during George's reign, the fall of the British Empire and the untimely death of the King himself at the age of fifty-seven.

The British people nevertheless rate the reign of George VI positively. The King won the sympathy of his subjects in the first year of his reign, and his wife played no small part in this. She alone knew how to help him become the ruler that he became.

For several days following the coronation, Elizabeth accepted to serve as patroness for a considerable number of charitable organizations, including the British Red Cross, the Royal Horticultural Society, the Royal National Lifeboat Institution, the Royal College, Cambridge University and many others.

---

8   Kenneth Rose, p. 103.

TOURING AS A WAY OF BOOSTING THE MONARCHS' POPULARITY

As we know, the British monarch rules over the state but he or she does not govern it. The monarch's main function is to boost the country's standing in the world and forge tighter bonds with other states. The new royal couple's journey across the country after their coronation won them great popularity. As the chronicles of those days show, in spite of the King being number one in the royal family, it was actually Elizabeth who most won the hearts of the people. Her predecessor Queen Mary had not been greatly concerned with public-relations efforts; she preferred to do her philanthropic activity at a distance. Elizabeth was very different, she won over the British population wherever she appeared. During World War I Elizabeth had lost one of her elder brothers and she always remained deeply concerned for veterans of that war. One of the first things that she saw to after becoming Queen was veterans. Here is what one said after speaking with her: "The queen asked me how I was getting on and wished me luck. She gave me a nice smile and a handshake. It was so friendly; it's taken twenty years off my age. She's lovely. I can't get over it."[9]

George VI and Elizabeth felt like a true king and queen after their triumphant state visit to France in 1938.

Not long before the couple received that invitation to visit their neighbours across the English Channel, the Countess of Strathmore – the Queen's mother – had died after a long illness. Three weeks after this sad event, the couple felt that they could now leave for Paris. The problem arose of what the Queen should wear considering that, on the one hand, she was bound for the world's fashion capital, and on the other hand, she had to show that she was in mourning. The King

---

9   *The Queen Mother: Her Reign in Colour* (Momentum, 2002) [on DVD].

himself decided on outfits for his wife. His sketches were based on female dresses of the Victorian era featuring crinolines. The modern tight-fitting dresses that were the latest fashion would not suit Elizabeth, who tended to be overweight. A choice that could not go wrong was made to use white for her apparel. White had been considered one of the colours of mourning in the royal family since 1862. This tradition had started when Queen Victoria's daughter Princess Alice was wed seven months after her father Prince Albert died.

The practical contribution that the British kings have made is more clear in international affairs than in domestic matters. Therefore, while the British people still felt a little uncertain about these two new figures on the throne, abroad, George VI and Elizabeth were received with open arms.

Thus, the year was 1938, France. The Parisians were delighted by the British royal couple, who walked hand in hand like lovebirds, and also by the Queen's original dresses. A number of photographs taken during this visit have been given to us. Even in photos, Elizabeth's regal beauty is striking. The French were astonished that after fifteen years of marriage, the couple behaved like newlyweds. This can be seen as being all down to Elizabeth, if we recall her devotion to the King, her cheerfulness, tact, ability to negotiate delicate matters and, of course, her sense of humour.

Meanwhile, the international situation was a disturbing one. Germany had strengthened its position, and it was clear that it was preparing for new conquests. In the event of a provocation by Germany, the United Kingdom would need strong allies at its side.

Thus, in May 1939 the King and his wife made a visit to Canada and the USA with the aim of strengthening the alliance with these countries. Elizabeth provided details of this trip in letters to her mother-in-law Queen Mary. Among other things, she mentions sailing past the spot where the *Titanic* foundered. In Canada they were greeted by crowds of thousands who had come out in admiration. The royal couple fearlessly went forward to meet them. Ordinary Canadians later rapturously described Elizabeth's lovely dark hair and impeccable dress. The country's intellectual elite were just as impressed and described the royal visit as follows: "Our monarchs are most remarkable young people. The queen has a perfect genius for the right kind of publicity."[10]

---

10   *The Queen Mother: Her Reign in Colour.*

One account of that royal visit comes from a Canadian veteran who had lost his sight in the war: "One thing I'll remember forever. The voice of the queen when she said, 'It is wonderful to meet you.' I sensed immediately that this was a real spirited and friendly hello. Their Majesties spoke earnestly to the person they were addressing. They have that faculty of putting you immediately at your ease."[11]

While they were abroad, the following episode took place. One little girl who dreamed of seeing "the real queen" with her own eyes, was disappointed that Elizabeth wore an ordinary dress like any mere mortal woman. The girl clearly expected to see the sort of queen that she had read about in fairy-tales. When Elizabeth heard of this, she insisted that the child be brought to her in the evening before Elizabeth went to attend a social function. The child was dazzled by the splendour of Elizabeth's truly queenly dress which shone with diamonds. The girl subsequently claimed that she had got to see a real fairy-tale queen.

As Elizabeth herself wrote at this time in a letter to Queen Mary:

> We have had a most touching reception everywhere – it has really been wonderful and most moving … Of course, they have no idea of our Constitution or how the Monarchy works, and were surprised & delighted to find that we were ordinary & fairly polite people with a big job of work. We have very long drives through the big towns, and I must say, we got very bored & tired, but both feel very well.

An amusing incident during the royal couple's visit is recorded in an account by Canada's Prime Minister, William Lyon Mackenzie King, who accompanied them on their tour of the country. Several times he insistently offered the Queen a warm cape, as it was quite chilly outside. The Queen however declined and told the Prime Minister that "she had woollies beneath".[12]

As for the royal couple's visit to the USA, they became the first British monarchs to visit the New World. World War II was on the horizon and the Americans sought to remain neutral. Elizabeth on the contrary called on them to unite against the looming Nazi aggression.

In early June the King and Queen arrived in Washington. The heat was sweltering, with local people dropping in the streets from

---

11   Ibid.
12   *The Queen Mother: Her Reign in Colour.*

heatstroke. Elizabeth again set down her impressions in a letter to Queen Mary: "We arrived in Washington in the most stupendous heat! I really don't know how we got through those 2 days of continuous functions mostly out of doors. However everybody was very very kind & welcoming, & made us feel quite 'at home'."

At first the people of the United States gave Elizabeth a cool welcome, blaming her for the fact that their fellow American, Wallis Simpson, had not become queen. The press was sceptical that Elizabeth would be able to win the Americans over, though they noted her jovial round figure and smile. In spite of pessimists' forecasts, Her Majesty acted, like always, carefully and managed to charm the Americans. Along their itinerary by train, the Queen went out to meet ordinary Americans and chat with them. Such actions required enormous bravery on her part, and the royals' bodyguards sometimes froze in horror, thinking that the enthusiastic crowd might swallow up their charges any second now. Such unusual interaction with the public helped boost the couple's popularity, and later the leaders of many other nations learned from these royals and began to use such mingling as a way to charm their populations.

A warm relationship was also established between the royal family and the US presidential couple, Franklin and Eleanor Roosevelt. The American First Lady later spoke highly of the Queen's elegant appearance, albeit without mentioning Elizabeth's keen mind, and said, "I was fascinated by the Queen. I do not see how it is possible to remain so perfectly in character all the time. My admiration for her grew every minute she spent with us."

At a reception at the British Embassy, Elizabeth fascinated those who were attending. One particular incident has stood out: one of the invited guests was holding in his hands cups of tea. Upon seeing Elizabeth, he exclaimed, "Oh, it's the Queen!" and dropped the tea. Her Majesty laughed and pretended that nothing had happened. She was simply capable of making so strong an impression on those who met her. From the newsreels that have survived from this time, we can see how thousands and thousands of Americans came out to see the royals' motorcade.

When the royal couple left the country, the North American press mused on the unusual success of this visit. George VI and Elizabeth had shown themselves well in the international arena and strengthened ties with the New World.

The royal couple returned to Great Britain feeling completely confident in their new role. Upon the triumphant homecoming, even their own subjects recognized that couple truly deserved to be on the throne.

World War II
(1939–1945)

Britain's secret weapon

The first years of the reign of George VI and Elizabeth coincided with some dark days for Britain. On 1 September 1939 Nazi Germany attacked Poland, a country which the UK had declared its public support for earlier. In response, the British government officially declared war on Germany. From this moment the popularity of the Queen, who was already well loved by the whole nation and the Commonwealth, began to soar.

In these anxious days George VI called upon the nation, old and young alike, to stand together in this hour of trial. In their exhortations of the nation, Western politicians often used apt quotations from Scripture. The King did the same on Christmas Eve when, overcoming his own fear of his stammer, he spoke to the people of Britain over the radio: "I said to the man who stood at the Gate of the Year 'Give me a light that I may tread safely into the unknown.' And he replied, 'Go out into the darkness, and put your hand into the hand of God. That shall be better than light, and safer than a known way.'" The King then added, "May that Almighty Hand guide and uphold us all."

Elizabeth too had weighty words for the nation: "War has, at all times, called for the fortitude of women. To us also is given the proud privilege of serving our country in her hour of need. It is, after all, for our homes and for their security that we are fighting. The call has come and from my heart I thank you."[13]

The war between Great Britain and Germany was somewhat different to the bloody battles that later raged on the territory of the USSR. The Nazis almost never clashed face to face with their opponent but rather assailed England by air and by sea. The eastern districts of London were hit especially hard by the German Luftwaffe. The London population soon began to be evacuated.

The scale of the danger in London during wartime is highlighted by the fact that the American ambassador in London, Joseph Kennedy

---

13   *The Queen Mother: Her Reign in Colour.*

(the father of President John F. Kennedy) urgently had his family evacuated to the continent and he himself, using the Christmas holidays as a pretext, left for America in early December, which forever tarred his reputation in the eyes of the British. When he returned to London after a prolonged absence, the miserable (in the words of the Soviet ambassador Ivan Maisky) government of Chamberlain had been replaced by that of the outstanding politician Winston Churchill. London gave the American ambassador a cool reception, as he was known for his anti-war views. At that time the United States witnessed widespread isolationist sentiment: many Americans felt that the war raging in Europe had nothing to do with them, and there were calls to keep out of the conflict with the growing fascist powers.

The British press excoriated Kennedy for "running away" to safety in the United States while the King and Queen, along with their daughters, stayed put under fire in burning London.

After this, a black mark was left on the elder Kennedy's political career. He was forced to tender his resignation to Roosevelt. The ambassador was never able to return to large-scale politics and vie for the presidency like he had planned. From then on he acted through his ambitious elder sons, setting them up to continue his dynasty and blaze their careers. John F. Kennedy managed to partially erase the stain of his father's apparent toadying to Hitler when, in 1944, his foolhardy pilot elder brother Joseph Jr. was killed in an aerial accident.

After war was declared, a strict blackout was instituted in Britain's towns and cities. In London the street lights were extinguished. The fencing around Buckingham Palace and other buildings was removed and melted down to make weapons.

In fear of a Luftwaffe attack, hundreds of thousands of Londoners hurriedly left the capital.

In 1940, when Hitler had taken nearly all of Western Europe, Elizabeth wrote to Eleanor Roosevelt:

Sometimes one's heart seems near breaking under the stress of so much sorrow and anxiety. When we think of my gallant young men being sacrificed to the terrible machine that Germany has created, I think that anger perhaps predominates. But when we think of their valour, their determination & their grave spirit, their pride and joy are uppermost in our minds. We are all prepared to sacrifice everything in the fight to save freedom.

Elizabeth and George VI, aware that their presence would support their compatriots' morale, began to visit factories and hospitals, the city's working-class districts and the bombed-out ruins. Day in and day out they made it their job to speak with ordinary Londoners and stoke courage in their hearts. Later, in a letter to Queen Mary, Elizabeth wrote that she felt like she had wandered through a dead city. There were ruined houses everywhere. Those buildings which had survived, stood empty. People had taken the bare essentials and left their homes in search of safety. But some had remained, and it was for their sake that Elizabeth continued to make her rounds. The visits lent people hope. Boosting the nation's spirit was now the most important task for her. Such meetings with the Queen strengthened her compatriots' faith in victory. Aware that her presence was important for their fighting spirit, Elizabeth regularly visited these places.

The Queen's attire for these visits was carefully chosen, even down to the smallest details. As mentioned before, she never wore black in these dark days, claiming that there was no black in the rainbow of hope. Thus, her dresses continued to feature only gentle pastel tones. Nor did Her Majesty give up her fine jewellery when visiting the districts of the lower classes. The Londoners, she explained, put on the finest clothing they had before they came to meet her, and so it would have been disrespectful on her part to wear something simpler. People who saw with their own eyes Her Majesty in all her splendour and heard her encouraging words, really were inspired. As for the King, from the very beginning of the war he put on a military uniform and continued to wear one until the final victory in 1945.

A large number of photographs have survived which depict the royal couple's visits through the East End which had been hit so hard by bombing. Buckingham Palace's press service took pains to inform the public about the royal family's charitable efforts and their visits. Such detailed coverage of the royals in the British press aimed to continually strengthen the monarchy's authority. The Queen Consort knew this better than anyone else. Among Her Majesty's own personal inventions in maintaining an image was (besides her smile and her fearlessness in meeting with the masses) her ability to play along with photojournalists.

After noticing the photographers at these visits which she made, Elizabeth would slow down so that they would manage to capture her with their cameras. If necessary, the Queen would repeat actions aimed at supporting the British population, urging it to come together, so that these actions could be turned into photos or newsreels. Her own style of posing for journalists is clearly visible when one looks at the old-time photos on the royal family's website. Elizabeth herself explained that she felt she had to give people an ability to do their job, as everyone at this time had their own job to do and the nation had to help one another.

The Queen did more than give words of encouragement to her subjects. Just like them, by staying in London under the bombing she too ran the risk of being buried in the rubble. The royal family's residence was targeted by bombing nine times. Remaining in London under siege grew more dangerous by the day. Churchill insisted that the Queen and the Princesses be immediately evacuated to Canada or another safe country. It was at this time that Elizabeth made her famous statement that has gone down in British history: "The Princesses would never leave without me and I couldn't leave without the King, and the King will never leave."

These words of hers swept across Britain and did more for the British people's hearts and minds than any inspiring speech. The royal family's presence in the city under mortal danger was of an immense significance for the fighting men. The British began to call the Queen their secret weapon. Hitler, an expert himself in stirring up the masses, called Elizabeth the most dangerous woman in Europe.

What did he mean by that?

In Viktor Popov's book on life at Buckingham Palace, the story is told of how the Queen Consort regularly came on the radio to address the people of various countries during World War II. She addressed the French with words of encouragement during the Germans' attack on France. Elizabeth also called on the Americans to join forces against fascism and come to Britain's aid. President Roosevelt applauded her for this.

What the urgings of men could not achieve, Her Majesty's charm could. It was precisely Elizabeth's popularity and her ever stronger influence on her subjects that worried Hitler. This was the exact opposite of the pro-German sentiments of the Duke of Windsor.

Elizabeth did not consider women's service in army units to be merely assisting men. She saw it as real military service, and the women were fighting for their lives just as much as the men. The Queen personally called on Britain's women to mobilize: "You have endured his bombs. You have helped to put out the fires that he has kindled in our homes. You have tended those he has maimed, brought strength to those he has bereaved. You have tilled our land. You have, in uniform or out of it, given help to our fighting forces, coping uncomplainingly with all the tedious difficulties of wartime. We are indeed very proud of you."[14]

After the war broke out, the Queen herself is said to have brushed up on her shooting skills. In fact, in the Strathmore family everyone had been brought up to learn to shoot well and they would apply their skills in hunting.

On 13 September 1940 George VI, who was at the time alongside his wife at Buckingham Palace, first heard the growing roar of German airplanes, and then from the window he saw the approaching Luftwaffe. The King did not waste time and, without a word, he grabbed the Queen and led her towards the exit. They barely managed to reach a safe distance and lay low when an explosion went off.

Several parts of Buckingham Palace were damaged. Elizabeth and George VI had stood only a hair's breadth from certain death. After having miraculously survived, the King said that he never wanted to come so close to death again. The Queen's reaction was different, "I'm glad we've been bombed. It makes me feel I can look the East End in the face."

For the Soviet ambassador in London, Ivan Maisky, who was an eyewitness to these events, it was obvious that the monarchy sought to use this to win the love of the nation and boost their own authority. In his diary during these days, he wrote:

> A few bombs were dropped on Buckingham Palace. No one was hurt, and the damage was quite minor. Nevertheless, the political effect has been colossal. The dynasty immediately acquired an aura around it. All through the city one hears: "The King is suffering with us, so how can we not suffer too?!" The British court, especially the royals, are grateful for what fate brought them. Years of painstaking propaganda on the monarchy's part could not do as much as the German planes' bombs. The royal couple did not refuse to leave the city after the bombing, on the contrary, they are visiting sites of major devastation in London on a daily basis. Moreover, the Queen has donated sixty sets of furniture from Windsor Palace's reserves for families which have suffered from the bombings. This has brought the pro-monarchy sentiments of the ordinary masses to a feverish apogee.

---

14 *The Queen Mother: Her Reign in Colour.*

All these things taken together have resulted in the population's morale remaining very high. Over the last two weeks, a gradual calm and normalization has set in. Football matches have been resumed, as have horse races and dog races. Cinemas and theatres continue to operate, though with limited hours. Yesterday Agniya and I were at the cinema. During the screening sirens went off – not a single person stood up and walked out of the room.

One thing is clear: the current level of the German military offensive is not enough to undermine the morale of the capital's population and the government.

Now the Queen could look not only her subjects in the face but also faraway Russia, where she had never been. How could she, as a member of the royal family, have visited Russia anyway, a country where the Romanovs – close relatives of the Windsors – had been shot? One episode is illustrative: in 1913 both august cousins, George V and Nicholas II, met in Germany at a wedding of their German relatives, and the British king noted that their mutual cousin Kaiser Wilhelm was jealous of how close the Russian and British families were.

As was mentioned earlier, during a time of mortal danger, the Romanovs had been left without any support from the British side. The Windsors had for a long time felt guilty because they had not responded to the Romanovs' appeal for help and they had not saved their kin from the violence of the Bolsheviks in 1918.

It was not until 1947, on the anniversary of their tsarist relatives' murder, that the UK Foreign Office sent a note of mourning, on paper with a black frame, to all diplomatic representations in London. In 1924, when relations were finally established between the United Kingdom and the Soviet regime, British protocol demanded that the Russian ambassador present his credentials to the Prince of Wales and not the King. Only in 1932 did the Soviet ambassador Ivan Maisky present his credentials to George V himself.

Elizabeth's influence as president of the British Red Cross

When the flames of World War II spread to Russia, the Queen began to make efforts to provide at least material support to these allies. Immediately after Germany's invasion of the USSR the British Red Cross, an organization in which Elizabeth served as president, sent seventy-five thousand pounds sterling of contributions to the Soviet embassy in London.

In his memoirs Ivan Maisky, without going into the Queen's personal monetary contribution to the Aid to Russia Fund, writes of how vital the Queen's authority was, as head of the British Red Cross, in spurring the rest of the population to contribute what they could:

> The first question was an organizational one. Who was to head this completely new branch of the embassy's work?
>
> ... Of course, it was possible to assign the Red Cross matter to one of the embassy secretaries, but that would immediately bureaucratize the whole thing and greatly dampen the public opportunities lurking within it ... In England, it is very common for women of high standing to serve as head of Red Cross funds. The president of the British Red Cross is not the King but the Queen.

For reasons of expediency, the ambassador followed the model of the British organization and assigned his wife Agniya Mayskaya to head the work of the USSR Red Cross at the embassy. In his opinion, appointing her would be consistent with English customs and opened up the widest opportunities for the Fund. As he wrote, "My wife, as ambassadoress, had connections and acquaintances that could be put to use for the Fund, beyond anything that the embassy's secretary or even advisor had access to. In what followed, my decision proved fully justified."

Thus, the enormous influence that the Queen had on her subjects as British Red Cross president became clear. According to the information which this organization provided to me, the Queen played an immense role in fundraising. Under Her Majesty's aegis, the British selflessly donated to various funds. In the autumn of 1941 the Aid to Russia Fund was founded under the Red Cross. It was headed by another Englishwoman of lofty status: Clementine Churchill. As Clementine wrote at the time in an appeal, reproduced in "The Grand Alliance" volume of Winston Churchill's history *The Second World War*, "Already the fund totals £370,000, and it is only twelve days old. Our gracious and beloved King and Queen, in sending a further £3000 to the Red Cross last week, expressed a wish that £1000 of their joint gift should be allocated to the Aid to Russia Fund. They have set a characteristic example."

However, the documents from the British Red Cross dating from October 1941 provide a contradictory account, and we will return to this subject now.

Clementine Churchill in Stalingrad (April 1945)

> Just as one candle lights another and can light thousands of other candles, so one heart illuminates another heart and can illuminate thousands of other hearts.
>
> Leo Tolstoy

The aid which the United Kingdom provided to Russia has been described in some detail by the eyewitness Ivan Maisky in his *Memoirs of a Soviet Ambassador*. Among other things, he talks about the first British people to offer contributions to the Russian soldiers through the Soviet embassy in London, and then how others took up this initiative and which eventually engaged Britain's highest authorities.

According to Maisky, aid to Russia began as a grassroots effort among Britain's ordinary people who traditionally felt a sympathy for the Soviet Union. It almost immediately reached such a scale that the government could only take it up and develop it further. Though the USSR's allies were still dragging their feet in opening a second front, they sought to provide moral and material support. One of the largest and most active efforts was the Red Cross's Aid to Russia Fund under the leadership of Clementine Churchill.

As Maisky states in his memoirs, when he spoke with Mrs Churchill in 1945, she recalled the birth of her celebrated Fund as follows:

> I was greatly troubled by the dramatic events which played out in your country after Hitler's invasion. I constantly wondered how we could help you. At that time, the opening of a second front was being widely discussed in Britain. I somehow received a letter from a group of women whose husbands and sons were serving in the British army. They insisted on opening a second front. "If these women are demanding a second front," I thought,

"that is, they are prepared to risk their loved ones' lives, then that meant that we should come to Russia's aid at once." I showed the letter to my husband. He replied that it would still be a long time before a second front was opened. This upset me, and I started to think about what we could do right now, immediately, in order to help your country. Then the idea of a Red Cross fund entered my mind.

Clementine's idea won active support from her husband and many prominent figures. In a short amount of time the Aid to Russia Fund became the British Red Cross's largest and most important effort during the war years. It was often referred to as "Mrs Churchill's Fund". Britain's population was quick to respond. Generous contributions, large or small, from individuals or groups, began to pour in from all over the country. Such an amount was raised that it surpassed the one million pounds sterling that had originally been aimed for.

However, at this time Russia did not need money, it instead required various medicines and equipment for field hospitals. Obtaining from the Soviet embassy a list of the most urgent items, procuring them from various enterprises, delivering them to ports and getting them loaded onto ships bound for the USSR – this all became Clementine's job day in and day out. Mrs Churchill was truly immersed in the work of her Fund and she did everything possible to ensure that medical supplies were shipped to the Red Army without interruption.

There were no special ships that could transport this humanitarian aid to Russia which had been gathered by various efforts. The goods had to be loaded onto Arctic Convoy ships alongside all the war materiel after agreeing with seamen and ministries first, and the effort had to work in close tandem with the Red Cross organization at the Soviet embassy in London headed by Ivan Maisky's wife Agniya. All this cooperation towards a common goal proved a great success.

In March 1942 the British Prime Minister suggested, with a smile, that his wife should be taken to visit the Soviet Union, as she had fully deserved it. "Just imagine!" Churchill said, "My own wife is completely sovietized ... All she ever talks about is the Soviet Red Cross, the Soviet army, and the wife of the Soviet ambassador, with whom she corresponds, speaks over the telephone and appears at demonstrations!"

In April 1945 the Soviet government, which had truly appreciated Mrs Churchill's work, awarded her the Order of the Red Banner of

Labour "for her outstanding service in raising funds in England in order to provide medical assistance to the Red Army".

But earlier, in the grim year of 1943, as Clementine inspected a warehouse in England where medicines bound for the USSR were stored, she decided that it would be good to show the British people what they had obtained through their own efforts and were sending to Russia. To do so, she organized an exhibition in the centre of London on 19 November.

During World War II the Arctic Convoys, in which military personnel from the UK and Norway served, delivered food and materiel to the USSR's Arctic ports. Over the war they provided, to this ally, seven thousand planes, five thousand tanks, as well as automobiles, fuel, rations, medicines, uniforms, iron and other raw materials.

In the 21 November 1943 issue of *Pravda*, it is written that Mrs Churchill had opened the Arctic Caravans exhibition in London, which informed attendees about – among other things – the first convoy which had journeyed to Russia back in August 1941. The newspaper's account was reprinted by the UK Russian-language magazine *Britansky Soyuznik* on 5 December 1943, where readers were told of why Mrs Churchill had been drawn to organize this expedition. The exhibition served as a visual manifestation of the aid which Britain was providing to Russia.

In a speech, Clementine explained that the medicines bought with the donations were not being sent on dedicated ships but were rather placed in whatever free space was available on the ships that were transporting arms. She also spoke of the difficulties which seamen on the Arctic Convoy ships had to overcome. They were constantly confronted by the enemy on the seas, underwater, and in the air, and in this they showed bravery and heroism.

Half a century later, in 1997, the Russian ambassador in London, Yury Fokin, began a tradition of decorating the surviving veterans among our allies of these Arctic Convoys. Below I describe in more detail how this tradition came about and what barriers had to be overcome in terms of obtaining an agreement, so that British veterans could be shown such recognition by a foreign state.

The organization which Clementine headed continued to work actively after the war ended and collect contributions from the British people. At the very end of these efforts, Mrs Churchill visited Stalingrad (among other Soviet cities) as part of a humanitarian mission for the Aid to Russia Fund. She brought enough medical equipment to equip an entire hospital.

According to Volgograd's Museum of Health Care History, this equipment was worth 816,099 pounds sterling. Also in the museum, is an exhibit dedicated to Clementine's visit featuring a photograph of her in the company of Stalingrad residents and Ministry of Foreign Affairs representative Fyodor Molochkov. Even today, a number of these items which Clementine Churchill brought survive: pitchforks for testing patients' hearing, a model for studying clinical anatomy, surgical pliers and other instruments. Some of these British medical tools are still being used.

After a tour of the city, Clementine met with workers at a tractor factory, she visited one of the renovated hospitals which had been equipped thanks to British donations, a new school, and the building on the Square of the Fallen Fighters where German Field Marshal Paulus had been captured.

What Clementine saw in Stalingrad left her deeply moved. In her book *My Visit to Russia*, which she wrote immediately upon her return to London and published in the same year, she writes:

> From Leningrad to Stalingrad. What an appalling scene of destruction met our eyes. My first thought was, how like the centre of Coventry or the devastation around St Paul's, except that here the havoc and obliteration seems to spread out endlessly. […] When one is in a city like Stalingrad the staggering loss of life and suffering produced by the Nazi aggression almost overwhelms one.[15]

Today, the Battle of Stalingrad Museum holds a copy of Lady Churchill's book, translated from English to Russian and published in London, with her autograph.

I would also like to mention another British woman in connection with the assistance provided to Stalingrad. This is Lady Rachel Workman MacRobert, who gave her support to a campaign raising funds for a new hospital in Stalingrad. This fearless woman was mother to three sons who perished in World War II while serving as pilots. Two of them were killed in air battles, while the third died in a plane accident. After Lady MacRobert was informed of the death of her sons, she immediately wrote to the UK Ministry of Aviation with a suggestion that it purchase a new bomber plane, and she attached a cheque for 25,000 pounds sterling to make it happen! Later, when the plane had been commissioned, it bore the name *MacRobert's Reply*. In her letter to the ministry, Lady

---

15   Clementine Churchill, *My Visit to Russia* (Hutchinson & Co., [1945]), pp. 28, 30.

MacRobert wrote, "It is my wish to make a mother's immediate reply in the way that I know would be my boys' reply – attacking, striking sharply, straight to the mark."

Later, in admiration of the USSR's heroic struggle, she donated another twenty thousand pounds sterling for a fighter wing, with the request that it should be used on the fronts where it could most help the Soviet Union. The fighters were named after her fallen sons: *Sir Alisdair MacRobert*, *Sir Rodereick MacRobert* and *Sir Iain MacRobert*. The fourth was dubbed *MacRobert's Salute to Russia*. Many Soviet mothers, moved by this woman's experience, wrote letters to her to express their thanks and support.

In our time, in the twenty-first century, an Englishman I know asked me during a tour of Volgograd, "Why do you have so many monuments to the war?" After over twenty-seven million people perished in the war, it seems obvious to me why we would memorialize them, but foreigners continue to be baffled. The defenders of the city who gave their lives, are now part of the Stalingrad landscape forever. Clementine Churchill foresaw this way back in 1945, when she wrote in her book, "Stalingrad was the turning point in the war, and that will be remembered by the Russians for centuries to come."[16]

What else does the world know about the city on the Volga besides the famous Battle of Stalingrad?

---

16   Clementine Churchill, *My Visit to Russia* (Hutchinson & Co., [1945]), p. 29.

A brief excursus into the history of the city on the Volga

I first saw Volgograd in late 1988. I left the airport and went straight through the entire city in the evening, all the way to its southernmost district, Krasnoarmeysky. Everything around me seemed majestic. Next to me stood a man whom I loved, a native of Volgograd and my future husband. The city which I was first laying my eyes on, would soon become my home.

I especially remember the unusually long road which was hung with festive lamps. I was not yet aware that Volgograd extends for a whole eighty kilometres along the Volga. As we travelled down the road, the gigantic symbol of the hero city, *The Motherland Calls* monument rose in the night sky. It was something I had only seen before in books or on television. Now, as I saw it first hand, illuminated by an otherworldly light (or perhaps it only seemed so to me), it towered over us and reminded me that I was now entering a legendary city.

The following year, 1989, was a significant one for Volgograd and a special one for me, because in February we got married and in November I gave birth to my son. The city rejoiced alongside me as it celebrated its four-hundredth anniversary.

Much later, after I had learned about the city's history and origins, I encountered contradictory information about when exactly Volgograd was founded. But after I studied numerous historians' claims and the evidence underlying them, I decided that I would go with the version stating that our city's founding can be traced to … Well, judge for yourselves.

Previously, the city bore the name Tsaritsyn. However, this proud name has nothing to do with the tsars. It simply reflects the Turkic name *sary-chin*, "yellow island". Or perhaps the name of the Tsaritsy River is the ancestor of the town's name Tsaritsyn, and again this is of Turkic origin: *sarysu* "yellow, turbid water". It is likely that the Slavic settlers, ignorant of the Tatars' language, simply liked the name and it took firm root for three centuries.

Until 1589 Tsaritsyn is not documented anywhere. We can only find mentions of temporary military posts on the lower Volga River. In his last will, Ivan the Terrible listed all of the towns and settlements which he was bequeathing, but there is no mention of Tsaritsyn. Only from 1589 does the name of our city finally appear in historical records. Among other places, it is mentioned in a charter of Tsar Feodor I in which he tasks some of his trusted men with building a fortified settlement on the "Yellow Island".

The founding of Tsaritsyn was dictated by the need to defend the Russian state's south-eastern borders from the incursions of the Sultan of Turkey and the Crimean Khanate.

Initially, this fortified town was founded on an island at the mouth of the Tsaritsy River, on a site where a smaller military outpost had previously stood. However, this location proved unsuitable for a fortress. First of all, the view was limited due to the high bank of the Volga River opposite. Secondly, the island did not offer any room to grow. Thirdly, the spring flooding of the Volga caused enormous damage. After a brutal fire in the late sixteenth century, the decision was finally taken to found the city anew on the right bank of the Volga.

From this, one finds it fitting that this city, which was intended, even before its founding, as a shield to protect the whole country from its enemies, completely fulfilled this destiny centuries later during the Battle of Stalingrad. This made Stalingrad a legendary city for the whole world. But more about that later …

In the interim, peace in the town was disturbed either by the peasant uprising led by Stepan Razin, or the Cossack Bulavin's revolt. Devastating raids by the Crimean and Kuban Tatars finally shook the town's defences. Strict measures had to be enforced, and in 1720 after Peter the Great visited, a powerful defensive line was built at his order. This line used the latest technology of the time and stretched from Tsaritsyn to the Don. Regular army forces and the Don Cossacks stood guard along it. The city, which was now so defended, began to swell with a civilian population.

After Russia's borders had expanded to the south, Tsaritsyn lost its strategic importance and became an ordinary provincial town. However, the building of the railway turned it into a sort of Russian Rome, as all of the roads in the country led here, along with the railways and waterways. It became a site for the transhipment of oil, fish, salt, wood and grain – all that the city was rich in.

The twentieth century brought a change in the political regime, and shortly thereafter the name of the city was changed to Stalingrad. Here I will briefly trace the life of the man whose name the city bore from 1925 to 1961.

The man Stalingrad was named after

As many people already know, Stalin (from the Russian *stal'* "steel") was not his real surname but instead followed the vogue of that era for pseudonyms, just like Lenin, Molotov, etc. The actual name of the man who would convince himself and those around him that he was made out of steel, was Joseph Jughashvili. Ethnically he was a Georgian and was born in the village of Gori on 9 December 1879.

Joseph's father, Vissarion, was a shoemaker who was inclined to drink and had a cruel and irritable temperament. Perhaps it was his father's influence – Vissarion's behaviour, lifestyle and unjust cruelty to his son expressed in frequent beatings – that moulded the character of the future dictator.

But an even larger role in the young Joseph's life was played by his mother. She was an ordinary washerwoman and toiled drudgingly all her life. She imagined a brilliant career in the priesthood for her son and encouraged him in every possible way to pursue this dream. Thus Soso, as the young Joseph was nicknamed, became a student at a religious seminary.

Though the young man was a good student, he would never graduate from the seminary. This period coincided with a wave of revolutionary fervour in the Russian Empire, and the young Georgian's rebellious spirit was drawn to it. He was subsequently imprisoned for revolutionary activities, his initial admiration for Lenin's mind and authority, as well as his first marriage. After Joseph's first wife died young, he was left alone with his elder son. As for Stalin's relationship with his second wife, it was precisely in Tsaritsyn where it first blossomed and ultimately led to marriage.

Thus we come to 1918. The Civil War was raging in Russia. Tsaritsyn had become a key point and all routes led to it, both over land and via the rivers. The city was thus an especially important position for the Bolsheviks. Moscow and Petrograd were suffering from famine. The central regions of the country had been cut off from Ukraine, Belorussia, Russia's south, Siberia and other important regions. There was a lack of food and fuel. Only from Tsaritsyn could grain and oil supplies flow. If this stream were cut off, the Revolution would perish from starvation and the cold. Everyone was well aware of this.

The Tsarist generals did their utmost to seize the city, while Moscow sought to hold it at any price and, moreover, boost the supplies of grain and fuel. To solve this matter of life and death, Joseph Stalin was sent there in June 1918 by the All-Russian Central Executive Committee on a mission of extreme importance. He brought with him Nadezhda Alliluyeva and her brother as a secretary and as another assistant, respectively. Stalin took direct and harsh measures to get transportation under control and bring Tsaritsyn's defence forces into line. Three offensive operations undertaken by the Tsarist generals (Krasnov, Mamontov, etc.) were unsuccessful and ultimately ended with a complete defeat at the hands of the Red Army. Grain and fuel now moved in full flow towards the centre of the country. Stalin had carried out his mission.

The Red Army's victory at Tsaritsyn allowed it to move to other fronts and go on the offensive. A campaign was launched against Denikin, Kolchak and other tsarist generals and ended with the enemy being completely crushed. In 1919 Tsaritsyn was awarded the Red Banner of Honour. It was against the background of these military activities that the forty-year-old Stalin and the eighteen-year-old Nadezhda Alliluyeva became man and wife. Two more children would be born to Joseph's second marriage: a son Vasily and a daughter Svetlana.

Stalin forged a successful political career. Lenin appreciated his loyalty and dedication to the Party and made Stalin his right-hand man. After Lenin's death, Stalin became the top-ranking person in the state and his authority grew steadily. To mark the fifth anniversary of the Defence of Tsaritsyn, the town was awarded the Order of the Red Banner. A delegation of local Tsaritsyn politicians who appreciated Stalin's role in the city's defence, asked Moscow to allow the renaming of Tsaritsyn to Stalingrad, a change which was carried out in 1925.

With regard to the Great Leader's family life, the Gordian knot of their tense relationship was tragically undone in 1932 by his wife's suicide. It is believed that Nadezhda Alliluyev was led to take her own life by her own disillusionment with regard to the ideals of the Revolution, disagreement with her husband's policies, his neglect and her jealousy. There is also an unlikely claim that Stalin himself shot his wife during a fit of violent rage during an argument. However, we are now straying from the topic of the present study.

Stalin never married again. His children were brought up by nannies and governesses. The later life of these children played out as follows: Stalin's elder son Yakov died while the Germans held him as a prisoner of war during World War II. However, Stalin refused to redeem him from Nazi captivity in exchange for the German Field Marshal Paulus. This man of cold steel explained his decision by saying, "I am not going to give up a field marshal for an ordinary soldier." Stalin's middle son Vasily was consumed by alcoholism from his youth, which eventually destroyed his health. He even ended up spending time in prison after his father's death. Stalin's younger daughter emigrated to the United States at the age of forty. This happened much later, in the meantime a battle was raging against fascism and victory ultimately came at an unimaginable price.

Some scholars have claimed that without Stalin, without his enormous power over the masses, this victory would never have come to fruition. This is hard to disagree with. Stalin's authority was great, and not only among the Russian population who lived under an information vacuum. According to Winston Churchill's memoirs, during a conference the Prime Minister decided that he would not stand up to welcome the Soviet leader. His high position entitled him to refrain from doing so if he wished. But then the charismatic Churchill saw for himself just how great Stalin's moral authority was. When Stalin arrived at the conference, the entire hall burst into applause, and some unknown force lifted Churchill up from his seat along with everyone else and made him greet the Great Leader of the Soviet Union.

Ambassador Ivan Maisky recounts a curious anecdote regarding a conversation he had with Stalin some years after the war. When Maisky noticed that Stalin was in an affable mood, the former ambassador ventured to ask him a thorny question. During his famous speech at a parade in November 1941, Stalin had told the nation, "The enemy is much weaker than some frightened intellectuals might think. And soon Germany will collapse under the weight of its own crimes." Stalin's words were famously taken to be the truth, and after this event people set off to defend their homeland, confident that they would be victorious. Maisky's question was: on what, did Stalin base his claim at that early and anxious period of the war? Stalin smiled and sincerely said, "I had no grounds for it. I simply had to rouse the people up somehow."

In this concise answer lies the key to Stalin's enigmatic personality: his ability to intuitively grasp what the masses' feelings really were in terms of morale, and then bring those feelings to where they needed to be. At all times great leaders have maintained power by having a keen sense for the signs of the times and knowing how to respond to them in a timely and appropriate way.

Stalin's sharp wit and his ability to anticipate change was noted by many of his contemporaries. Vyacheslav Molotov tells of a Politburo session in 1944 when Soviet forces were pushing through Europe. Here, Stalin again anticipated how things would play out, and he spoke of the need to train new diplomatic personnel for peacetime. When someone objected that everyone trained in the humanities had already been drafted into the army, the Great Leader suggested that young engineers should be sent to train at the Diplomatic College. One of the many former engineers who emerged as an outstanding diplomat at this time was Anatoly Dobrynin.[17]

In fact, Anatoly Dobrynin has pointed to another example of Stalin revealing great strategic thinking during difficult negotiations.[18] On the eve of the Potsdam Conference, President Truman wished to put pressure on Stalin and make him more amenable during the looming negotiations, so he told Stalin about the Americans' new atomic bomb. In response Stalin, a skilled politician, simply thanked his counterpart for the information. Truman assumed that Stalin simply did not understand what a threat this new weapon was. In fact, after this brief conversation Stalin immediately ordered that the Soviets work harder and faster at creating their own atomic bomb. The American president's attempt to put pressure on Stalin proved futile.

We must also credit Stalin for the fact that the norms of a fair trial were observed at Nuremberg. It was Stalin who insisted that those who had committed crimes against humanity be handed over to an international court. Meanwhile, the British for example, suggested that those men should simply be executed.[19]

In 1956 the 20th Congress of the Communist Party of the Soviet Union was held. At this event, the cult of personality that the late Great

---

17   Yury Kashlev, *Diplomaticheskaya akademiya MID Rossii: istoria i sovremennost'* (Moscow, 2004), p. 79.

18   Yury Dubinin, *Masterstvo peregovorov* (Moscow, 2009), p. 130.

19   Oleg Troyanovsky, *Iz kogorty vydayushchikhsya diplomatov* (Moscow, 2010), p. 104.

Leader had established was condemned. As a result of this, Stalingrad was renamed Volgograd.

Nevertheless, everyone continued to refer to the city as Stalingrad, and there are many foreigners today who are still not aware that this famous and heroic city has got a new name. It is noteworthy that when a delegation from Volgograd met with the Queen Mother in London in April 2000, the honourable lady referred to the city on the Volga as "the former Stalingrad" or "the city which formerly bore the name of Stalingrad".

Recently, there have been calls to restore Volgograd to its previous name. One of the arguments for this is the legendary victory in the World War II confrontation known to the world as the Battle of Stalingrad.

Through the prism of an honorary sword of King George VI

A short path to victory lies in everyone showing victory.

*Inscription on a memorial plaque offered
by the town of Wallis, Wales, UK to Stalingrad in 1944*

Volgograd, in the early twenty-first century. The Battle of Stalingrad Museum. In one of the numerous rooms where gifts and tributes from around the world are held, I examine a relic that speaks volumes.

I am looking at a sword, a shining steel blade. The handle is woven with gold. Along the edges of the silver hilt, lions' heads are laid. The impressive length of this sword (1.2 metres) and the gold and silver inlay on its scabbards (complete with a star, a coat of arms and a monogram) lead one's thoughts back to the era of kings and queens.

Where did this unusual gift come from? The answer can be found right on the blade itself, acid-etched: "TO THE STEEL-HEARTED CITIZENS OF STALINGRAD, THE GIFT OF KING GEORGE THE SIXTH, IN TOKEN OF HOMAGE OF THE BRITISH PEOPLE".

This sword asks us to rewind the tape of history back to World War II. In 1939, hostilities broke out between the United Kingdom and Nazi Germany. Winston Churchill, as head of the government, wanted to find solid allies. Among these were the USSR and the USA. Therefore, when Hitler's Germany attacked the USSR, this was the most important event for the UK for the last two years. Now, Albion had a precious ally in the Soviet Union.

On 22 June 1941, Churchill addressed his people over the radio and said:

> [Hitler] wishes to destroy the Russian power because he hopes that if he succeeds in this he will be able to bring back the main

strength of his army and air force from the East and hurl it upon this island … His invasion of Russia is no more than a prelude to an attempted invasion of the British Isles … The Russian danger is therefore our danger and the danger of the United States …

Thus, Britain stood on the USSR's side in the Soviet–German war, and by helping the Soviet Union, the British would also be saving themselves. Yet in spite of this loud and bold proclamation, for a long time the opening of a second front remained mere words.

Ordinary British people, unhappy with their government's sluggishness, showed their solidarity with the Soviet people by donating to the Aid to Russia Fund. In the autumn of 1942, Stalingrad's fight for survival was headline news in the war for the whole world. The British followed, with bated breath, these developments on the Volga. The outcome of the Battle of Stalingrad was of decisive importance not only for the USSR and Germany, but also for the UK. It was through Stalingrad that the Germans could have laid their path towards Baku and its oil fields, and then on towards the oil fields of the Near East (which Britain relied on for its energy needs). When the Soviets proved victorious at Stalingrad, the British were jubilant. The Soviet soldiers' victory, the British saw as a victory for themselves too. And the pain of Stalingrad they felt as their own.

Proof of this solidarity between the Allies was clear in the Arctic Convoys that brought rations, medicines and warm clothing from Coventry, London, Manchester and Sheffield, to Stalingrad during the grim war years.

In the UK National Archives, there is a file dedicated to what Britain should do as a token of recognition for Stalingrad. Amazingly, this was drawn up before the Battle of Stalingrad had even ended, namely on 24 September 1942, when correspondence arrived at Downing Street, addressed to Churchill, with a suggestion that Stalingrad should be decorated for its bravery regardless of the outcome of the battle.

In the UK it is the custom that outstanding people and events are recognized with awards, precious gifts and lofty titles. For the British themselves, it is a high honour to be awarded such a decoration. The most esteemed awards are granted by the royal family. For example, the monarch's private secretary, after many years of faithful service, is usually given the rank of lord. Elizabeth II has knighted nearly all of the Prime Ministers under her reign.

The UK Foreign Office received an enormous number of letters from ordinary people who were touched by the bravery which the people of

Stalingrad showed as they withstood this onslaught. From the steady stream of appeals to the government and from the newspapers' editorials, one could see that British solidarity was running unusually high. For example, the British pointed to the island of Malta, which had been awarded the George Cross. A reaction to British society's unanimous sentiment came in October 1942, as correspondence circulated within the government with regard to what token of recognition would be suitable for Stalingrad. The George Cross was not considered appropriate, however, as it was not intended for foreigners and foreign cities. The Military Cross, which was awarded to the French at Verdun, was proposed as an alternative.

The document reflecting these discussions is dated 19 November 1942, the very day when Soviet forces began their offensive at Stalingrad, which subsequently led the USSR to victory. The British only learned about this later, however. In December 1942, *Pravda* reported that a new military decoration had been created for the defence of Stalingrad. This announcement once again sparked among the British people calls to somehow recognize the city on the Volga, and there were discussions about forging medals from gold, decorating them with diamonds, and so on.

It is generally typical for the British to be so meticulous when it comes to any honours. For example, Kenneth Rose, author of a biography of George V, has written of how long and painstaking the process was of choosing the exact crown which the King would wear before his Indian subjects in 1911–1912.

Thus, in the best English tradition, the debate on the most appropriate way to recognize Stalingrad was drawn out, and only in late February 1943 did Churchill finally approve the recommendation that this heroic city be awarded a ceremonial sword as a gift from the King.

In February 1943 George VI consented to Churchill's proposal and issued a decree that a kingly sword be prepared as a gift to Stalingrad.

The sword was forged at Wilkinson Sword by the old and esteemed British master Tom Beasley, who came from a long line of swordsmiths. By this time Beasley was eighty-three years old, and in his own words this blade was the finest he had ever forged, though he had already forged weapons for five British monarchs. In an old black-and-white newsreel held at the Battle of Stalingrad museum, the master swordsmith, without even turning away from his forge, claims that he has put everything he has ever learned from the age of eight (the year he started out) into this gift to the people of Stalingrad, whose hearts he felt were truly made of steel.

On 21 February 1943, the King sent a telegram to Mikhail Kalinin, Chairman of the Presidium of the Supreme Soviet:

> It was the unyielding resistance of Stalingrad that turned the tide and heralded the crushing blows which have struck dismay into the foes of civilization and freedom. To mark the profound admiration felt by myself and the peoples of the British Empire, I have given commands for the preparation of a Sword of Honour, which it would give me pleasure to present to the city of Stalingrad. My hope would be that this gift might commemorate in the happier times to come the inflexible courage with which the warrior city steeled herself against the powerful and persistent onslaughts of her assailants, and that it might be a token of the admiration not only of the British peoples but of the whole civilized world.

The Chairman of the Presidium of the Supreme Soviet sent a telegram to King George VI in reply on 23 February 1943:

> I ask Your Majesty to accept my most sincere gratitude for your gift, which represents such a high appraisal of the Red Army's achievements in the battle against our common enemy. The British people's numerous manifestations of their friendship towards the Red Army serve as testimony to the firm alliance between our countries. I have informed the Stalingrad municipal authorities of your decision to award this city the Sword of Honour forged at your command which will doubtlessly be accepted with gratitude both by the defenders of Stalingrad and by the people of the entire USSR, as a symbol of the brotherhood in arms between the peoples of the United Kingdom and the Soviet Union.

Before the sword was sent off to Stalingrad, the British had an opportunity to admire this gift from the King, destined for that city which had proved victorious. The sword was placed on public display in Coventry. Money was also raised there for a charitable fund to assist Stalingrad. Gradually, bonds were forged between two cities that had suffered a similar fate, Stalingrad and Coventry.

I should also note that a similar offering to Russia had already been made by King Edward VII. A kingly sword was presented to Nicholas II in commemoration of the English king's visit. That gift bears the English inscription "For His Imperial Majesty Emperor of All Russia Nicholas II from His Loving Uncle Edward Reval 1908", and it is kept today in Tsarskoye Selo. Of course, these two gifts meant very different things.

In time, when the sword ordered by George VI had already been forged and had arrived in Stalingrad, it was put on display, among other such gifts, for all honoured visitors of Stalingrad. The famous American writer John Steinbeck held it in his hands. He wrote down his impressions of this royal gift in his *A Russian Journal*. In this book, the great writer recounts rather callously his 1947 journey through a USSR where the destruction of the war was still evident. When Steinback visited Stalingrad, where, at an unimaginable toll, the course of the war had reversed, he showed the smugness of a man who had never witnessed fighting firsthand. Steinbeck criticized the lofty personalities of those who made such useless gifts and suggested that half a dozen bulldozers should be presented instead so that Stalingrad could more easily be cleared of all its rubble. Apparently he only had a superficial understanding of events and writes of the defenders of the city, "They were little people who had been attacked and who had defended themselves successfully".

That history was different, later generations of Stalingraders know from the documentation of the war, the sculptures and memorials, as well as the memoirs of those who are able to distinguish courage in others, because they themselves possess it.

In 1999 in the Imperial War Museum's park in London, a Soviet memorial was erected for the over twenty-seven million Soviet people who perished in World War II. This monument was the work of the talented Volgograd sculptor Sergei Shcherbakov. Previously an identical sculpture, resembling a mournful female silhouette holding a bell over her bowed head, had already been installed near Volgograd in the village of Rossoshki, where fierce fighting took place in the autumn of 1942. In the centre of the memorial stands the statue of the "Mourning Woman". On either side of it stretch long rows of military gravestones with soldiers' names, dates of birth and the same last date for everyone: "42 ... 42 ... 42 ... 42".

How many of our boys were laid to rest here? A bell tolls for them and the lives they were robbed of. Those who have come after the war, after the destruction it wrought, have no doubt that only great people, with great spirit, are capable of such a great victory.

This is confirmed in the account of Ivan Maisky, who visited Stalingrad in the autumn of 1943:

> The city lay in ruins ... Only here, face to face with these consequences of the great battle, have we begun to better understand and grasp what happened here just a few months ago, what incredible will, strength, energy, decisiveness and dedication one must have needed to live through all this, withstand it and then smash the cruel enemy.
>
> We left Stalingrad deeply shaken by the great historical drama that unfolded here, and also inspired by the new life springing up which we encountered at every step among those sacred ruins.

We can also look through the chronicles of World War II. Tehran, November 1943. The leaders of three Allies against Hitler's regime have come together for a conference: the USSR, USA and Britain. The main item on the agenda is finally opening a second front in Europe, an opening which had already been postponed multiple times. It was precisely at this time, during this historic meeting in Iran, that Churchill handed the King's sword of honour to Stalin.

Valentin M. Berezhkov, an interpreter with the Soviet delegation, passed over in his memoirs the fact that due to a hand injury which Stalin had received in his childhood, Stalin dropped the sword at this solemn instant. However, footage shot during the event captured this episode.

At the Moscow Kremlin on 2 February 1944, on the anniversary of the final routing of Nazi German forces at Stalingrad, the sword was handed over to a delegation from Stalingrad. D. M. Pigalev (representing Stalingrad) accepted the King's gift from Marshal Semyon Budyonny with the words: "By accepting this sword, we declare that we will keep it as a symbol of the budding military cooperation between the peoples of the USSR and the United Kingdom."

At the same time as this ceremony in Moscow for handing over the sword, the Soviet ambassador to the UK, Fyodor Tarasovich Gusev, held a reception in London for the English master craftsmen who had been part of the sword's making. They were invited to the Soviet embassy in London and there, each of these eighteen men, received a personally-dedicated photo album with scenes of Stalingrad before, during and after the battle. The album for Professor R. M. Y. Gleadowe, who was responsible for the sword's overall design, was handed over to his widow.

Some feel that the new Soviet ambassador, who had arrived to replace Ivan Maisky, was incapable of establishing such a trusting relationship with Churchill as his predecessor Maisky had done. When Maisky was recalled to Moscow from London, this caused some consternation among the British leadership, who had enjoyed a good rapport with Maisky and admired his wit, his intelligence and his diplomacy. When Churchill was informed that Gusev had been appointed the new ambassador, the Prime Minister was hurt. He met with this "newcomer" only on very rare occasions, when strictly necessary.

What caused this unexpected change of diplomatic staff on Moscow's part?

Here is what Stalin himself had to say about it: "We were forced to recall Ambassador Maisky, who has been too quick to justify the actions of the British as they sabotaged the opening of a second front in Europe." Later, when Churchill praised ex-Ambassador Maisky, Stalin replied that Maisky talked too much and did not know how to keep his mouth shut.

Stalin's suspiciousness is well known. It is possible that under these circumstances, his rotation of ambassadors anticipated later observations in the field of diplomacy. The famous Russian diplomat Viktor Popov has noted that in diplomatic jargon today, one speaks of "localitis" in reference to a diplomat long resident abroad becoming too sympathetic to local interests and acquiring a sort of pride in the place of his or her assignment.[20] There are objective grounds for this: it is assumed that after many years of living far away from one's native country, a diplomat loses touch with his or her own people, comes to side with the country of assignment and ceases to identify its flaws.

Even if we accept that Ambassador Maisky came involuntarily to love the country he was living in, we certainly cannot deny the vital work he did as a diplomat. One needs to only look at his memoirs to get a sense of this man's authority, superb mind and role in facilitating Soviet–British cooperation. Maisky's firm position with regard to the UK Foreign Office has also been mentioned by the Russian diplomat Oleg Sakun, who points to a telegram, later published, from the US ambassador in London and dated 13 June 1941, that is, shortly before Ger-

---

20 Viktor Popov, *Sovremennaya diplomatiya* (Moscow, 2003) p. 490.

many attacked the Soviet Union.[21] In this telegram it is mentioned that the Soviet ambassador had been confidentially informed about the huge concentration of German forces on the Russian–German border.

Churchill, too, valued his relationship with Ambassador Maisky: they often met, discussed the course of the war and planned the opening of the second front.

Over Churchill's long and active life, a great many politicians strove to win Churchill's respect. Biographies mention Churchill's admiration of the young John F. Kennedy, and in connection with this they describe an episode from their first meeting on board Onassis's yacht. Kennedy tried in every possible way to get the esteemed politician's attention, but it had no effect on Churchill. The American then expressed his disappointment to his wife. Jacqueline Kennedy looked at his creased suit and quipped, "I think he thought you were a waiter, Jack."

Here are Maisky's curious parting words as ambassador:

To be fruitful, ties have to be living and active. Fruitful ties are frequent meetings for work and outside of work, showing friendship, inviting the other party to the theatre or to lunch. Wishing them a happy birthday or sending them some interesting book. Maintaining such ties requires time and effort. They cannot be neglected for long. They must constantly be fledged.

I look at the King's sword through the glass and through the decades, and I try to understand the true meaning of this gift. This sword presented to us was a recognition of our victory, as well as a recognition of our growing authority abroad. And of course, this gift was a sign of natural admiration for the victor!

Today this sword of honour (just as old as the Victory at Stalingrad) has one more meaning: to strengthen the bonds of friendship between Russia and the UK. In 1990 Volgograd was visited by Princess Anne (the Queen Mother's granddaughter). She also visited the museum and held her grandfather's ceremonial sword in her hands.

In 1967 this gift from George VI was displayed at a joint English–Soviet exposition in London. In 1979 Londoners had the opportunity to see it again at the USSR Industrial Exhibition. In 1982, in a number of UK cities – London, Sheffield, Manchester, Glasgow, Edinburgh, Liverpool and Coventry – the work of the English master goldsmith

---

21   Oleg Sakun, *Diplomaticheskoye remeslo* (Moscow, 2007), p. 206.

and silversmith Leslie Durbin was exhibited; Durbin was responsible for the decorations on the famous sword. Among his creations that were displayed, this honoured gift to the people of Stalingrad received the attention it deserved. One imagines that this was certainly not the last visit that the King's sword made back to its birthplace.

Operation Moonlight Sonata and Coventry

For the people of Volgograd, among all the cities of the world, Coventry holds a special place as its twin city. This small English town evokes the same warmth and affection in me as well. On several occasions I have visited this place at the invitation of Gary Crookes, Lord Mayor of Coventry, in the period 2013–2014. Yes, he served but a single year, for such is the head of the city's traditional term in order to avoid corruption. The fates of my own city, Volgograd, and the English town Coventry are closely intertwined. It was an especial honour for me to receive a letter from Lord Mayor Gary Crookes as recognition for my part in strengthening ties between the twin cities of Volgograd and Coventry.

I shall briefly sketch the history of this town over the last millennium. Today, it is mainly known for the chic Jaguar cars, as the headquarters of this auto brand is located precisely here. Coventry is linked with a touching legend about a real-life person, Lady Godiva. You can see her commemorated everywhere in the city: numerous statues, music festivals in her honours, paintings and tapestries depicting her, as well as pamphlets and souvenirs.

Lady Godiva went down in history not only as a wealthy landowner around Coventry, but also as a lady of great compassion who stood up to her husband for the local people and persuaded him to reduce his exorbitant taxes. The Lord agreed on the condition that his wife, famous for her modesty, ride naked across the entire town. Lady Godiva did this nevertheless, though only after warning the townspeople that they ought to stay inside their homes on this day. The sole curious onlooker, who was nicknamed "Peeping Tom", was struck blind when the Lady came by on her horse.

Gary Crookes, with whom our delegation from the Russian embassy struck up a warm friendship with, arranged for us a tour of the city and he himself told us of the most illustrious episodes of the town's history.

Especially interesting was St Mary's Guildhall, where once the Scottish Queen Mary Stuart was imprisoned at the order of Queen Elizabeth I. We visited this stone room with an extremely low entrance and heard that this doorway had been specially designed so that the unsubmissive Queen would be forced to kneel.

Another interesting site was St Michael's Cathedral, which was destroyed during World War II. The following episode from this period is linked with this church: the people of Coventry – as residents of one of Britain's industrial centres, managed to get used to attacks by German planes. On the night of 14–15 November 1940, the air-raid sirens went off yet again, and many people did not even leave their homes to go down into the bomb shelters. They were unaware that German command had decided to launch a campaign of terror and level their town to the ground, thus sparking panic among the workers at the nearby plants. This deadly German operation was code-named Operation Mondscheinsonate (Moonlight Sonata). In wave after wave, 509 Heinkel bombers dropped their deadly loads onto the town.

In a single night, a city with a thousand years of history was destroyed. Of its twelve airplane factories, only rubble remained. Also destroyed was the town centre, famous for its architecture dating back to the fourteenth and fifteenth centuries. The death toll from the bombing stood at five hundred people, and figures indicate that over a thousand were wounded.

After the tragedy, on 16 November, King George VI and Queen Elizabeth came to visit Coventry in order to show their support and determine what help the townspeople needed. During this period of German bombing of English communities, we know Elizabeth's pain at seeing such destruction and human grief from her letters:

> It really makes one wild with rage to see all the insane destruction of beautiful and often dearly loved buildings. To think that so much beauty should be sacrificed to Nazi brutality is horrifying. The destruction is so awful and the people so wonderful – they deserve a better world.[22]

Immediately after the tragedy in Coventry, an emergency committee was set up to distribute funds meant for the suffering people of the town. Assistance came in from the state, from the municipality and from indi-

---

22 *The Queen Mother: Her Reign in Colour.*

vidual donators. If they so wished, the most defenceless segments of the population – children, the elderly and women – were evacuated.

The royal couple's visit made a lasting impression on the inhabitants of Coventry and emboldened them. The Nazis did not achieve their goal: instead of panicking, the next day the townspeople resumed production at the surviving military factories. Over time, the number of raiders in their swastika-decked bombers fell as the Germany army turned its attention to the USSR.

But not everything is so transparent regarding Coventry's "Moonlight Sonata".

Let me cite the suggestion of researcher Anthony Cave Brown, who in the 1970s was one of the first to examine British intelligence's archives after they were partially opened. In his view, Winston Churchill, as head of the UK's wartime government, already knew about the looming bombing of Coventry two days beforehand. Codebreaking experts at a secret facility in London had warned him about the Germans' plans. However, the government took no measures to strengthen defences around the city and to evacuate its population, so that the Germans would not discover that their codes had been broken.

Cave Brown's accusation caused a firestorm in the press, but Churchill's reputation was later restored in the official history of British intelligence. Authors claimed that the government had indeed known in advance about an imminent German operation, but the experts could not determine the exact date or target for the attack.

More recently, when I met with another Lord Mayor of Coventry, Jack Harrison, I asked him: did the Prime Minister know about a looming attack? The English mayor confirmed that this was true, and he explained how vital it was for the wartime government to take this dramatic step. Back then, in 1940, British intelligence had put a lot of work into deciphering German communications, so that they could ultimately deliver the Germans a powerful blow. In order to keep the enemy complacent, the British government had to sacrifice Coventry for the sake of the final victory against the Nazis.

In 1942, when the defenders of Stalingrad were making an enormous effort to hold off the enemy's assault, this news from the Eastern Front came as a sadness for the people of Coventry. Everyone understood where the outcome of World War II was being decided.

On 23 August 1942, the enemy's air force carried out a barbaric bombing of Stalingrad that involved two thousand plane sorties. The skies were lit up by the flames from oil burning on the Volga. The city lay in ruins. Nevertheless, its defenders did not give up, and word of their great feats reached Coventry as well. It seemed so similar to what they had been through earlier.

On 16 September 1942, Coventry's mayor, Alfred Robert Grindlay sent a telegram to Stalingrad:

> Coventry most warscarred city in Britain solutes with profound admiration the supremely heroic city of Stalingrad whose defiant stand against a common enemy stirs every heart. The people of Coventry with memories of Nazi savagery burned on their minds cherish for you in Stalingrad feelings of special sympathy and rejoice in your wonderful courage and iron resolve to fight on to victory.

On this piece of paper, yellowed by time, the story of the friendship between these two cities begins. A message sent in the same year by Coventry workers testifies to their feelings of guilt to the people of Stalingrad:

> We realise that the Soviet people's resistance to the Nazi beast and their innumerable casualties have saved us from the horrors that we had merely anticipated during raids on our city in November 1940. We are sending our delegate to the British Parliament in order to demand that our country fulfils its obligations with regard to the USSR. Comparing Russia's war efforts with ours should shame us and we should act quickly and resolutely.

It was in Coventry, in the ruins of the cathedral, where the sword of honour gifted by George VI to Stalingrad's defenders was exhibited. According to the mayor, for the people of Coventry this sword is a symbol of heroism and triumph. Thus, in 1944 the initial work towards a twin cities relationship was carried out. In fact, the entire twin cities phenomenon was born with this friendship between Coventry and Stalingrad, with this example then being taken up around the world.

Today in Coventry, in the square outside the Anglican cathedral, a bronze sculpture has been placed that shows Satan bound and, over him, the winged archangel St Michael holding a spear, a reminder of Nazism defeated. In Volgograd one finds a Coventry Street, and one of the squares in Coventry has been named after Volgograd.

The subsequent friendly relationship between these twin cities has been described by Yury Tumanov in his book *Stalingrad and Coventry*. I would only like to mention how, in the peaceful post-war years, delegates from each city have visited the other, and joint events have been held where ordinary citizens from both towns could interact. In 1986 a joint effort was organized against the proliferation and use of atomic, chemical and other weapons of mass destruction.

In 1944 workers at a Coventry textile factory, through the Women's Anglo-Soviet Committee, sent Stalingrad a linen tablecloth and sixty pounds sterling of assistance. The centre of the elaborate tablecloth was colourfully embroidered with the signatures of eight hundred and thirty women who had raised these funds and also the words "A little help is better than a lot of pity" and "So dear the land that gave you birth and dearer yet the brotherhood that binds the brave of all the Earth". Among those who made their contribution to the tablecloth was Miss Pearl Lilley who later, in 1970, visited Volgograd as the secretary of the British Soviet Friendship Society.

In the autumn of 2004, the Battle of Stalingrad Museum organized a joint exhibition together with Coventry's Herbert Art Gallery and Museum. On this occasion, the idea was suggested to create a "virtual tablecloth", an online version of the one which the women of Coventry presented to Stalingrad in 1947. On a special website, anyone who was so willing could "embroider" their own name, along with a message to the inhabitants of the twin city.

In 2009, the tablecloth story got a sequel when a Volgograd seamstress, over many months, embroidered a tablecloth of her own for Coventry which featured gathered signatures, and on the sixty-fifth anniversary of the towns' twinning this second tablecloth was bestowed to Coventry by a grateful Volgograd.

In our peaceful era, this second tablecloth got a great deal of attention. Let me cite just one commentary: "The tablecloth made by K. is embroidered with greetings from the mayors of a great many towns and regional authorities. This all looks rather artificial, not from the heart but just checking the boxes. Her sole job was to make a tablecloth."

Underscoring that the problem of too much fuss and formality existed before this, we can quote some regrets of Russia's ambassador to the UK, Victor Popov, in his book about Elizabeth II during her visit to Russia: "The embassy limited the guests at the reception to such a degree that few people were invited who actually knew England, loved that country and could meaningfully communicate with the royal couple."

Nevertheless the English, a polite people, treated this gift carefully, and during one of my visits to Coventry I had the opportunity to see the tablecloth exhibited in the town's museum.

With regard to the meaning and value of the friendship between the twin cities, let me mention just one more aspect by which the British side has traditionally orientated itself and which, in their opinion, testifies to how fruitful these ties have been: the economic aspect. Throughout the ages, the UK has found economic figures on both sides to be a barometer of the success of cooperation with foreign cities and countries. Thus, on the part of the people of Coventry, one often hears calls to boost relations between the two cities so that they not only exchange Christmas cards, but also attract international business to one city or the other.

Duelling snipers during the Battle of Stalingrad

How was the victory at Stalingrad reached? I will mention just one example out of the myriad incredible feats displayed during the battle: Soviet sniper Vasily Zaytsev's killing of hundreds of Nazis and his duel with a champion shooter on the German side. This story later inspired the Hollywood film *Enemy at the Gates*.

Stalingrad under siege, 1942. Vasily Zaytsev, a young man originally from the Chelyabinsk region with its vast forests and wildlife, has arrived, at his own request, so that he can wipe out the enemy in the place where the very outcome of World War II is being decided – Stalingrad. He was young, but in his own words he was quite ready to face the enemy. Like in everything, if one wants to achieve success, one needs to train hard. Young Vasily Zaytsev had that training.

His grandfather Andrei Zaytsev, an ardent hunter, took great care to teach Vasily the art of hunting from the latter's childhood: how to read animal's tracks like a book, how to follow wolves and bears by these tracks. Andrei taught his grandson the main skill that a hunter must have: to stand motionless for hours awaiting an animal, without ever giving off one's presence, allowing the animal to come so close that it could be put down with a single shot. Vasily quickly matched his grandfather's skill, and with time he learned to lie in ambush so quietly that even his mentor could not spot him until the young man spoke up.

Initially Vasily went hunting with a bow and arrow, but after his first successes his grandfather gave him a real shotgun and shot for different types of animals. He also gave his grandson some words of advice: don't ever waste a shot, shoot without missing and drop the animal with the first shot. Vasily was twelve years old then.

At the age of fifteen Vasily went to the town of Magnitogorsk to study at a high school for construction workers. After he graduated with honours, he completed an accounting program and began working in this field. Soon the quick-witted young man was appointed as a senior insurance inspector. In 1937 Zaytsev left to serve in the Pacific navy, and he was there when the war broke out. He was then called into the army to defend his homeland – and Stalingrad.

Here his hunting skills came in handy, namely being able to drop an animal with the first shot. The number of Nazis he killed reached dozens, and then hundreds. Vasily Zaytsev's name became legendary across the entire front. But his greatest trial and glory still lay ahead.

Rumours eventually reached Berlin of this sharpshooter taking down the German assailants one after another at Stalingrad. The Third Reich decided to send its own best shooter to take Zaytsev down. This was the European shooting champion and director of a German sniper school – Major Erwin König.

König was secretly transported by plane to the city on the Volga. Soon, Soviet soldiers began to pay for even the slightest mistakes with their lives. It was obvious that a master killer was at work. Then, through German POWs, Soviet intelligence managed to learn that the hunt was on for their own Zaytsev. A deadly confrontation began between these two renowned snipers. Now they both had to determine the other's location and enter into a showdown from which only one of them would come out alive.

During the siege of Stalingrad, Zaytsev not only took down Nazis with precision, but he also taught his skills to his comrades. According to his doctrine, pinpointing a target in the enemy's camp was a two-stage process. First, one had to study the enemy's defences. Medical orderlies proved a great help with this, as they could describe the layout of the terrain and the history of where and when soldiers were wounded. Zaytsev was thus able to determine exactly where the opponents' guns were trained. The second stage was searching for the actual target. In order to avoid falling into the Nazi sniper's sights, Zaytsev had to reconnoitre using a trench periscope or looking through an artillery tube. The sniper could not use the sight scope on his rifle or his binoculars, because the reflection emanating off them would give him away. A sniper who does not know how to carry out his observations undiscovered is no sniper at all, only easy pickings for the enemy. There was one more important rule: in places where the enemy was formerly active, and where no movements are observed at all, a skilled predator is surely lying in ambush.

This is how Zaytsev described his position:

I had already learned how to quickly identify the signatures of the Nazi snipers. By means of their shooting and their camouflaging, I was able without much difficulty to distinguish the more experienced shooters from the novices, and the cowardly from the stubborn and decisive. However, the character of the head of their school long remained a mystery to me.

In Zaytsev's account, their daily reconnoitring brought no clear results. It was even impossible to determine where the Nazi sniper's general position was.

Zaytsev opposed maintaining a constant position himself. A sniper, he felt, ought to be mobile, capable of appearing suddenly in places where the enemy least expected him. Soon Zaytsev realized that Köning was also changing position frequently and just as meticulously trying to sniff Zaytsev out. However, to gain the initiative, Zaytsev had to make an effort. How could he outwit his opponent, draw him into a complex battle and tie him down in a good position?

One day, during the Stalingrad siege, one of Vasily's comrades said "There he is!" and stood up for a split-second. This was enough for the poor soldier to be hit. Clearly the shooter had been a veteran sniper.

On the fourth day of this standoff, Zaytsev's assistant, in order to tie the opponent down in a place where Zaytsev could shoot, made a false shot. Everyone then waited for the position of the sun to shift, so that the enemy's optics, not their own, might give off a reflection. Finally, something glimmered at the far end of a sheet of scrap metal. Kulikov – Vasily's comrade – raised his helmet on a stick. The Nazi immediately reacted by firing off a shot. In order to put on a convincing show for the enemy, Kulikov slightly showed himself, screamed and fell down.

This strategy worked. The German popped out from the scrap metal in order to ensure that he had hit his target. But it was him who was put down instead, with a single precise shot, like always, by Vasily Zaytsev. Later, this triumphant sniper and his comrade Kulikov hauled their slain foe from under the sheet of scrap metal, took his documents and brought them to their division commander.

Zaytsev wrote in depth and engagingly about his struggle with the German champion in his memoirs. The name of this acclaimed Russian sniper has entered the pantheon of honoured citizens of Volgograd. In 2000, on the fifty-fifth anniversary of Victory Day, this list was expanded to also include Elizabeth Windsor The Queen Mother. I will discuss the recognition she received from the city in a separate chapter.

With regard to Vasily's subsequent life, he fought through the whole war before he was ultimately wounded. Mikhail Kalinin himself placed the Hero of the Soviet Union medal on him. In Berlin, he left his own inscription on the walls of the Reichstag. Zaytsev lived to a ripe old age and was buried, at his own request, on Volgograd's 102-meter Mamayev Kurgan height, a place that he and his Soviet comrades refused to surrender to the enemy.

The great Soviet victory at Stalingrad was initiated by feats such as Zaytsev's. The British people's relationship to the warrior city was expressed in musical form in 1943 as the song "The Voice of the City", by the famous English composer Elizabeth Maconchy, a graduate of the Royal College of Music, to words written by Jacqueline Morris, a pupil at a girl's school in South Wales.

> I have been dreaming
> of my city
> my city as it was there
> long years ago. My
> sleep was short but my dream has given me strength [...]
> Our lovely buildings crumble.
> Our gardens are black and bare. [...]
> There is a broken heart in Stalingrad. [...]
> Yet the voice of our city calls to
> us, Strengthens our weary limbs, Will inspire us to
> bravery. Until, one day, we shall wake – With
> signing in our hearts [...]
> Happy and strong again, Stalingrad, Stalingrad
> Happy and strong again [...]

At the time, this piece was dedicated to suffering, and when Stalingrad enjoyed great popularity in Britain. Today, the sheet music to this song is held in the Battle of Stalingrad Museum. Unfortunately, our foreign allies initially had little faith that the USSR would win, and they long delayed opening a second front in Europe. But the legendary triumph of the Red Army in this battle on the Volga inspired the fiery hearts of the British people and the calculating minds of its government. Thus, the prevalent opinion about the balance of forces on the Soviet–German front changed and convinced the UK that the time was right for the solution we all needed: opening a second front to help the USSR.

Her Majesty Queen Elizabeth The Queen Mother (from 1952)

George VI exits

After the victory in World War II, the reign of George VI and Elizabeth saw fireworks and festivities. In spite of the post-war devastation and Churchill's resignation, the royal couple continued to enjoy unusual popularity. The bravery they had shown during the war strengthened the monarchy's authority among the British people. In February 1947, the royal family made a tour of South Africa.

The central event of this journey was to be the opening of Parliament in Cape Town. However, the royal tour aimed to convince the dominions that the United Kingdom was just as strong a country as ever. The royal family's tour ultimately lasted four months and covered ten thousand miles. This would be the last royal-family tour before the heiress to the throne announced her engagement. The person accompanying the family in South Africa, Field Marshal Jan Smuts (Prime Minister of South Africa, 1938–1947) spoke of how important their visit to the dominions was, saying that it had a much larger effect than he expected. According to Smuts, the local people were truly interested and there was lively interaction between the royals and the locals, instead of the traditional stillness, where the royals remain mysterious and aloof. The local people were touched by the attention shown to them.

In reality, not everything went so smoothly during this period. Britain's economy had a hard time recovering after the war. George VI felt exhausted, which is visible from the documentary evidence of the journey. The Queen's worries at the time were expressed in a letter to her mother-in-law, Queen Mary:

> This tour is being very strenuous and doubly hard for Bertie, who feels he should be at home. We think of home all the time and Bertie has offered to return, but the prime minister thought that it would make people feel that things were getting worse.

This is a very difficult and anxious time, and the British people seem to be taking it magnificently.[23]

When one reviews the documentation of the royal visit to Southern Africa, one feels an involuntary sense of fear for their lives. Imagine a handful of white people surrounded by hundreds of indigenous Zulus, barely clothed with animal skins and armed with bows and arrows. They shouted their battle cry and showed off their rituals and dances and shook their spears. Gradually, the anxiety abated. With this show, the tribes greeted the King and Queen and expressed their pleasure at the royal visit.

When this trying multi-month tour had come to an end, George VI looked back on it as follows:

It was a wonderfully friendly welcome given to us by all in South Africa. It has given me a new outlook on life after those terrible war years in Britain, which to me were a period of great strain, and followed by the life of austerity which we are compelled to undergo as a result of our exertion in the war. I have been able to relax for a bit, and feel that I shall now be able to return to my work in London with renewed energy.[24]

However, the King's hopes for renewed vigour were disappointed, for his health took a drastic turn for the worse and he was now in the last years of his reign.

On 12 May 1947, the tenth anniversary of Their Majesties' coronation was celebrated. On 15 August of the same year, India won its independence. George VI was no longer Emperor of India, and Elizabeth went down in history as the last Empress of the United Kingdom and the British Commonwealth.

The end of the British Empire may well have affected Britain's position in the world, but it did not disrupt the harmony within the royal family. On 20 November 1947, an event of incredible grandiosity took place: the wedding of Princess Elizabeth, heiress to the throne, to Prince Philip, a love story I will touch on further. On 26 April of the following year, the twenty-fifth wedding anniversary of the reigning couple, George VI and Elizabeth, was celebrated at St Paul's Cathedral. Unlike

---

23 *The Queen Mother: Her Reign in Colour.*
24 Ibid.

subsequent generations, Elizabeth and George VI remained a model couple to the end.

On the day of this silver jubilee, George VI addressed the nation by radio. He spoke of the strength and energy which his wife had given him all these years. He told his subjects of how happy he was with his family, thanked his wife for her support and… began to gradually leave the stage, increasingly handing the royal duties over to his eldest daughter. The King's health steadily declined, which some have ascribed to his long smoking habit. Doctors discovered that he had lung cancer and there was no hope of recovery. His incurable illness was kept a secret, even from Princess Elizabeth, for she was awaiting her firstborn child (the future Prince Charles) and nothing was to darken these days for her.

On 11 December 1951, George VI and Elizabeth marked the fifteenth anniversary of their coronation. Three days later, the King celebrated his fifty-sixth birthday, which was to be his last. In late January 1952, the royal family set off to see an American musical, after which Princess Elizabeth and her husband, the Duke of Edinburgh, left for Australia. The King saw them off at the airport and waved goodbye to them for the last time. On the photographs taken of this scene, George looks haggard and sad, as if he knew that he was seeing his daughter for the last time.

On 6 February 1952, George VI died. In Britain, crowds of people came out onto the streets to say farewell to their king. While Elizabeth was mourning the death of her beloved husband, Churchill gave a speech to the nation to pay tribute to her. "Our hearts go out tonight to that valiant woman," he said, "with famous blood of Scotland in her veins, who sustained King George through all his toils and problems, and brought up with their charm and beauty the two daughters who mourn their father today. May she be granted strength to bear her sorrow."

When the Queen Mother stepped away from supreme authority, she did not escape the fate of one who was reluctant to hand over such august powers to a new person, even if it was her own daughter. At first she even refused to give up the royal residence, where she had lived with George VI for some sixteen years. Young Elizabeth II did not dare object to her mother, but then Parliament intervened and reminded the dowager queen that these suites in Buckingham Palace were traditionally intended for the current monarch. Somewhat hurt, the Queen Mother retired to her native Scotland, where she acquired Mey Castle and, in order to fill the void in her heart, got down to thoroughly renovating it.

What feelings did Elizabeth, sent away from her position of authority, experience in this period? We can point to an analogous example from 1837, involving the Duchess of Kent, when her daughter, the famous Queen Victoria, ascended to the British throne. Hitherto, as the mother of the heiress to the throne, the Duchess enjoyed considerable influence and even dictated to the young Victoria the positions she must take. But as soon as Victoria was crowned, the first decree she issued was that her sleeping quarters be separated from her mother's. Subsequently, the young monarchess made a complete break with her mother and all state matters were decided without consulting the Duchess.

Here is how Stratchey describes the Duchess of Kent's position in this period of transition:

> She found herself, absolutely and irretrievably, shut off from every vestige of influence, of confidence, of power. She was surrounded, indeed, by all the outward signs of respect and consideration, but that only made the inward truth of her position the more intolerable. Through the mingled formalities of court etiquette and filial duty, she could never penetrate to Victoria. She was unable to conceal her disappointment and her rage. "*Il n'y a plus d'avenir pour moi*," she exclaimed to Madame de Lieven, "*je ne suis plus rien.*"

A century later, the widowed Elizabeth wrote to a friend during these doleful days, "It is very difficult to realize that the King has left us [...], and I really thought he was going to have some years perhaps less anguished than the last fifteen. [...] He was so young to die, and was becoming so wise in kingship. He was so kind too [...]. Such sorrow is a very strange experience – it really changes one's whole life [...]."

As the widowed Queen stepped aside from the throne to make way for her daughter, she did not wish, in accordance with her natural lust for life, to take a mourning title as her predecessors had done. After all, another widowed Queen was still alive, Mary, the mother of George VI. For this reason, Elizabeth began to be called Her Majesty Queen Elizabeth The Queen Mother. Why "Mother"? Because she was the mother of the reigning Elizabeth II.

Thus, Elizabeth divested herself of the duties of Queen Consort, which she had brilliantly fulfilled for sixteen years. Once, during World War I, her mother-in-law, Queen Mary, who had dedicated all her time and effort to caring for the wounded and thus showing an example to the other royal-family members, heard one of them complain, "I'm tired, and I hate hospitals!" The stern Queen curtly replied, "You are a royal, and we never grow tired, and we love hospitals."

In this lies the key to the question of how to be queen. It was not just childhood dreams that turned Cinderella into a queen. Elizabeth became worthy of her position through responsibility, tact, political foresight, generosity and humanity.

In a sense, one might call Queen Mary the maker of queens. Not only did Mary inculcate in her young and inexperienced daughter-in-law the rules of royal etiquette, but she also helped bring up her granddaughter, the present Elizabeth II. Here are some of her simplest and most famous teachings on how to dress, taking modern fashions into account: a queen should always dress in such a way that even in a crowd she stands out; black is only for mourning; the most appropriate colours are lemon, emerald, violet and so forth; a queen should wear a hat that sets her apart from the crowd; her coiffure should be similarly distinctive, and visible both under her hat and under her crown. It is precisely for this reason that British queens maintain the same convenient hairstyle over the decades.

Soon, as it turned out, Queen Mother Elizabeth's political experience proved useful, and vital for her elder daughter. The widow of George VI, due to her energy and popularity, could not remain aloof from her role and responsibilities as a royal family member, and she again accepted the burden of serving as patroness for numerous organizations. She also made official tours through the Commonwealth nations, and thus strengthened the ties between them and Britain.

In 1953, the Queen Mother and Princess Margaret headed for Southern Rhodesia, to open an exhibition there. Altogether, she made thirty-eight official visits abroad with the aim of strengthening the bonds between the dominions and Britain. One of her most memorable tours was her jubilee visit to Canada in 1989, where the Queen Mother was greeted by crowds of admirers. She had made her first visit to Canada exactly fifty years earlier.

In her new role, the Queen Mother became someone to whom Elizabeth II could turn to for advice and, the British press claims, for many years she was the unofficial head of the Windsor family.

Elizabeth II

For the present book, Elizabeth II is an especially interesting figure because her life is so closely linked with the life of the Queen Mother. Moreover, she became the first British monarch in four hundred years to set foot on Russian soil.

Unlike her father George VI, who took on the role of monarch unexpectedly, Princess Elizabeth had been groomed for the throne from childhood. From birth she was the third in line to the throne (after her uncle Edward VIII and her father George VI). She was brought up correspondingly and the future queen studied history, constitutional law, geography, literature, art, music, French and other subjects. She was schooled at home by the best teachers in Britain.

There is a saying: "The ruling class is prepared from childhood". Indeed, the education of this future head of state was more thorough than a school. The heiress had to study the basics of economics, legislation and constitutional law. Her mother, Elizabeth, and grandmother, Queen Mary, gave her lessons in court etiquette.

There were also lessons in equestrianism, as the future Queen would eventually have to be present on horseback at military parades and other solemn occasions. At one point, one of Elizabeth's older relatives had given her the following advice: "Go riding, it will make you very popular with the people! Every English person loves horseback riding." All British monarchs have a love for horses, but Elizabeth was especially passionate about these stately and powerful creatures.

In her childhood, her favourite presents were a wooden horse, a book about horses and later a pony. The Queen rode well in her time, she has a fine knowledge of thoroughbreds and she loves to feed horses. Only in these brief movements can she truly be herself, and not the Queen.

Moreover, Elizabeth speaks daily with the chief authority for horse races and can identify, at once, the future winner. She can easily determine how honed a horse is and what its chances for success are. How did she manage to develop these skills?

In a television program, a famous English expert on racehorses described how he could flawlessly identify a future race winner, even while it was still a colt, by its look and by its desire to dominate and be number one. A modest horse, in his view, was a second-rate one. In general, it is not only the British aristocracy that has shown an interest in thoroughbred racehorses, but also the elites of many other countries.

Elizabeth's constant companion in childhood was her younger sister Margaret. The girls went everywhere together, and they would even wear the same outfits. However, their personalities were totally different. The heiress to the throne, aware from an early age of the burden of responsibility, was a serious, focused and compassionate young lady. Margaret, on the other hand, was free of such cares and responsibilities to her people, she behaved much more freely and was more outgoing, and she could immediately attract the attention of those around her. One thing is curious: according to the accounts of her contemporaries, the elder Elizabeth's presence was rather oppressive for her elder daughter. The latter would fall silent when her mother entered the room. Elizabeth II did not complain when her mother refused to give up Buckingham Palace, which was intended for the reigning monarch. In later years, when the Queen Mother spent beyond her Civil List means, due to her love for horses and dresses, Lilibet never reproached her mother in the slightest. As the publicly available accounts suggest, in the Queen Mother's last years, Elizabeth II gave her two million pounds sterling of her own money so that the elderly lady could continue to maintain her aristocratic lifestyle.

Why did the Queen Mother, such a smiling woman and so beloved by all, cause her daughter to be so demure? It probably lay in the fact that the elder Elizabeth only showed her kind and generous side to outsiders. Those who dealt with her closely, on the other hand, called her "an iron fist in a velvet glove". She was not capable of forgiving and forgetting. Lilibet was a witness to how her mother dealt with Edward VIII after he gave up the throne. In their home, Edward became someone who should not be spoken of. The Duke of Windsor was *persona non grata* at events involving the royal family. All other members of the royal family were forbidden to visit him. The Duchess of Windsor never got the title of Her Majesty that she sought. When Edward made his first official visit back to his homeland in 1952 for the funeral of George VI, he found himself the target of all the Queen Mother's wrath. She publicly blamed him for his brother's untimely death, for if George had not had to take on the burden of the kingship, he might have still been alive.

The elder Elizabeth truly suffered from the loss of her husband. A photograph has been given to us of the funeral of George VI that captures the three queens: the dowager Queen Mary, Elizabeth II and the Queen Mother. The Queen Mother's face, under her veil, is racked by true grief. We should not forget that she had not only lost her husband the King, but also her status and a portion of her power and influence. Had that not been what the daughter of a simple earl had wanted since her very childhood?

Lilibet took great care of her mother, but she harboured no illusions about the old woman. According to one of the girls who served with Princess Elizabeth in the Women's Auxiliary Territorial Service during World War II, the royal couple once arrived to inspect their unit. The heiress's fellow servicewomen, who were drawn from all social classes, noticed a hostile expression on the Queen Consort's face, as if to say "What kind of lowly girls has my daughter fallen in with here?". For the girls, this was very hurtful and repugnant, and importantly, the Queen Consort was nothing like the smiling and good-natured woman whom the press usually depicted.

Thus, Elizabeth had some reason to be so restrained with regard to her mother. She could sense that her mother was a talented actress, and she knew how powerful her famous smile was. The former Princess and present Queen herself, has always been distinguished by a natural air and a refusal of theatricality. Is it not because her august position came to her trouble-free, she inherited the queenship without any competition and she had never been forced to win and hold onto her throne?

There is one more important difference between the two Elizabeth's. The mother loved society life, balls and galas. She could easily maintain small talk. Her daughter on the other hand has always preferred solitude, and when among society she has always carefully considered what to say before speaking. She takes more after her taciturn father, and their mission has been the very same: to bring the nation together under the monarchy. And when it comes to love, the younger Elizabeth has been just as faithful as her father the King. For her, a marriage has been once and for life.

Nevertheless, the Queen Mother, with her smile and her skill at making her charitable deeds known in the press, was perennially adored by the nation. On numerous occasions the royal family has hid behind her, especially at times that were critical for the monarchy.

When the younger Elizabeth turned fourteen, World War II broke out. There was a curious coincidence in this: her mother Elizabeth had turned fourteen when World War I began.

The Princess, inspired by the work done by her parents, did not hesitate in getting involved in the common cause. A photograph has survived of the young Elizabeth in military uniform changing a truck wheel under the guidance of an instructor. I have already written about life in the royal family during the war years, but on the eve of the war, one more important event took place: the heiress to the throne met her future husband Philip.

Philip, Princess Elizabeth's chosen

Philip, Prince of Greece, was born in 1921. Though both of his parents were of royal blood (his father was Prince Andrew of Greece and Denmark and his mother was Princess Alice of Battenberg), his family was badly off. His parents' marriage was fragile and would ultimately collapse, and as a child, Philip was left to his own devices. It was his numerous aristocratic relatives who saw to his upbringing and education, and he spent time living with them in various countries.

This hard upbringing forged the young man's character and taught him that he could not rely on anyone but himself. For some time he was a pupil at a preparatory school in Britain, where disciple was strict. However, Philip never complained. When he was older, he said that it was strict discipline that makes a boy into a man.

The period he spent attending school in Germany coincided with the Nazi dictatorship. Even then, Philip dared to mock the Nazis' behaviour, suggesting that their custom of giving the raised-arm salute was like a pupil asking his teacher for permission to leave the room. For his anti-Nazi convictions and his open lack of respect, the young prince was sent from Germany back to England. After Greece, Britain is seen as his second homeland.

As mentioned above, Philip, from childhood, was distinguished by a sense of leadership. In 1939, he became a cadet at the Naval College in Dartmouth (the alma mater of George VI, Princess Elizabeth's father). After graduating he served first on the HMS *Ramillies*, then on the HMS *Valiant* and on the HMS *Wallace*, where he was present during battles against Germany, Italy and Japan during World War II.

Princess Elizabeth and Prince Philip made each other's acquaintance on 22 June 1939, right before the war. Of course, they had met earlier as small children, for example, at the coronation of George VI, where many of their high-born relatives were present. But now, when Elizabeth was thirteen years old and Philip eighteen, this encounter proved the beginning of a closer relationship, and ultimately love. Here is how it happened: on this day the royal family visited the Naval College in Dartmouth. They were met by Lord Mountbatten, Philip's uncle. According to some authors, Lord Mountbatten was the one who introduced the heiress to the British throne to Prince Philip. Dickey, as Lord Mountbatten was nicknamed among his close peers, was a remarkable figure. He was related to the British royal family, but due to his German background, after World War I he found himself to be an unwelcome guest with George V. Dickey was a close acquaintance of Edward VIII until the latter's abdication, but then he went over to the winning side, that is, George VI, who valued Lord Mountbatten, especially for his qualities as a businessman. However, the Queen Consort had little trust for this relative's sly and crafty qualities.

Let us return, however, to the moment when the Princess met her future husband. Philip was called upon to start a toy railway for Princess Elizabeth and Margaret. Philip did not think this a serious pastime, and he invited the girls to the park to play croquet and tennis. In fact, he really wanted to show off his sporting abilities, and he succeeded in making an impression on the young Elizabeth, who occasionally uttered her admiration aloud. It was obvious that the Princess was interested in her distant relative. But what about the Prince?

The following episode says it all. When the royal family sailed from Dartmouth on their yacht *Victoria and Albert*, they were escorted out of the port by the cadets' boats. Philip's skiff kept going, alone, boldly towards the open sea. The Princess watched him with binoculars, but the King was alarmed and demanded that this daredevil be ordered, by radio, to turn back.

Soon after these events I have described, Britain entered World War II, but the two youngsters continued to correspond. In 1943, they met again. Now, Elizabeth was seventeen years old, and it soon became clear to everyone that the Princess was in love. She hung a portrait of Philip in her room, and in speaking with others she often referred to his opinions about things.

Meanwhile, Lord Mountbatten was cautiously exploring whether it might be possible for the heiress to wed his nephew. George VI however, was in no hurry to offer his daughter's hand. Then, Dickey began an indirect attack: he suggested to Philip that he accept British citizenship. Philip did understand how important British citizenship could be, but he was very upset at his uncle's intrusion into his personal life. In time, Lord Mountbatten came to understand that the meddling of others was pointless, for the Princess was already in love and dreaming of marriage.

"After the war, things will probably unfold of their own accord," he suggested, while talking with relatives.

One cannot say that the King and Queen were overjoyed at this turn of events. They were aware that Princess Elizabeth would eventually become leader of the nation, and the requirements for any suitor were strict indeed. Passionate love alone was not enough. Kings are not always able to marry for love, and the sad and infamous story of Edward VIII and Wallis Simpson serves as testimony to this. The Princess's parents told their love stricken daughter their objections: firstly, she was too young to get married, and secondly, Prince Philip was of German background – after yet another war with Germany, marrying him would be unpatriotic. After all, George V had torn up his German roots in 1917 and changed the royal family's name from Saxe-Coburg to something more authentically English: Windsor. This new name was taken from Windsor Castle, the founder of which was William the Conqueror.

The Princess responded with her own arguments in favour of the idea. Firstly, she loved Philip, and he was the only man whom she had ever loved. Secondly, her father (George VI) had married for love, and her mother, *née* Elizabeth Bowes-Lyon, was not even of royal blood while Philip was. Thirdly, because of love her uncle King Edward VIII had abdicated and now Elizabeth, if she were forbidden from marrying the man she loved, was prepared to follow her uncle's example.

When we look, today, at the utterly composed Elizabeth II, it is hard to believe that such passions raged within her in her youth, and she was even capable of turning down the throne that was hers, for the sake of love!

After weighing up the pros and cons of this argument, the King and Queen set the following condition for their daughter: they would give their consent to Elizabeth and Philip's marriage after Philip had turned twenty-one. Meanwhile, Philip was urged to refer to himself solely as Lieutenant Philip Mountbatten, so that his non-English origins would be forgotten.

Early in 1947, the royal couple and both princesses set off for South Africa, where they spent four months. While Princess Elizabeth was lovelorn, her chosen one far away, her younger sister Margaret struck up a friendship with Group Captain Peter Townsend, who was accompanying their retinue, and their relationship then became a romantic one.

Like in a fairy tale, the two lovers, Elizabeth and Philip, withstood all their trials, and on 9 July 1947 their engagement was announced. Their wedding was held at Westminster Abbey on 20 November of the same year. King George VI was deeply touched by this ceremony, but he also felt a loss, because his elder daughter was leaving the family home in order to start one of her own.

After marrying Princess Elizabeth, Philip received the title of Duke of Edinburgh, which he still holds today. As far as the Duchess was concerned, after the death of her father in 1952, she ascended to the throne under the name of Elizabeth II. An unusual situation arose by which three women had the title of Queen at the same time: the youngest and reigning Queen Elizabeth II, the Queen Mother Elizabeth and the dowager, Queen Mary.

Prince Charles – the direct heir to the British crown

The presently reigning British monarch, Elizabeth II, bore four children: Prince Charles, Princess Anne, Prince Andrew and Prince Edward. Prince Charles, who was the Queen Mother's darling grandson, came into the world on 14 November 1948. He is well known among the public due to his tangled relationships with the women in his life: Princess Diana and Camilla. But first and foremost, Charles is the first in line to the British throne, and therefore, he has been a target of constant attention from the British press and everyone else. Since the moment he was born, the media has put every step and slipup of his under a microscope. Even when he was sent to a public school as a boy (earlier heirs to the throne were educated at home), journalists camped out with notepads and cameras, wherever he went. Elizabeth II was forced to ask representatives of the press to leave this special schoolboy in peace and let him get a traditional education, just like other British children.

As is clear from the numerous biographies of Prince Charles, his childhood was not a very happy one. As his upbringing was entrusted mainly to nannies, governesses and his grandmother (the elder Elizabeth), he felt lonely and suffered from a lack of attention and tenderness from his mother. Even more painful was the criticism he received from his father, the charismatic Duke of Edinburgh. The Duke, as we recall, coped splendidly with the difficulties that his childhood brought, he easily gained authority among his peers during his school years, and he was a great achiever and never a complainer. How disappointed the Duke must have been when his eldest son, the heir to the throne, showed precisely those qualities which Philip felt were a sign of weakness: Charles was too sensitive, unable to make friends easily and introverted. Prince Charles also lacked the dashing good looks of his father. His prominent ears were often a target of mockery in the press. However, the Prince of Wales still had his following of fans, and they shrugged off this criticism. Moreover, Charles was largely able to overcome his quiet nature and achieve success in sports which require courage: car racing, flying fighter planes and helicopters and polo.

All in all, Charles received a fine education. At Cambridge he studied history, architecture, environmental science and other subjects. He continued his education at an institution in Australia and entered the Naval College in Dartmouth, which many male members of the British royal family have passed through before him. Charles is considered to be the most educated of the royals. Now as heir, the Prince has focused his efforts on the following things: solving issues of unemployment, youth education, business, the environment and architecture. Charles was responsible for the book *A Vision of Britain: A Personal View of Architecture* (which even got a Russian translation in 2005). He has founded numerous charities, including one for educating underprivileged youth from around the world. Once, in the era of Margaret Thatcher, the government criticized Prince Charles for his too hands-on approach to the problem of unemployment. Of course Prince Charles is so interested in the problem of unemployment, they snidely claimed, after all he himself is unemployed.

The most tender issue in Charles' life has been his failed marriage to Princess Diana and his long-running affair with the married Lady Camilla Parker Bowles. With regard to the Prince and Russia, he has made several visits to Saint-Petersburg and the Solovetsky Islands for the usual reasons royals visit: to visit famous places, contribute to charities and establish ties with the country visited.

A LOVE TRIANGLE: CHARLES, DIANA AND CAMILLA

When setting aside the story of Queen Mother Elizabeth for a moment to touch on her close circle, one cannot overlook the relationships that her grandson Prince Charles has had with certain women. Here is why: as we recall, in 1936 Queen Elizabeth and her husband King George VI ascended to the throne thanks to the abdication of Edward VIII. This newly-crowned Queen could hardly have imagined that decades later, her own beloved grandson and crown prince would prove just as vulnerable to the charms of an unsuitable lady.

Let us draw an analogy. The loves of both Princes of Wales have been loudly chronicled through the twentieth century. The romance of Edward VIII has already been described. With regard to Charles, his weakness for the female sex matches his predecessor.

Thus, in 1981 the world stood rapt in front of their television screens to watch the wedding of the heir to Britain's throne and his lovely young bride Lady Diana. The nation approved of the future king's choice and forgave whatever flaws he might have shown in the past. The monarchy's authority and popularity again soared to record heights.

The reason why the crown prince put off marrying for so long was the same as it had been for Edward VIII. For a decade the Prince had been in love, and the feeling was mutual, but the target of his affections was a married woman with two children: Camilla Parker Bowles.

Back when they had first met, however, his love was still a free woman. The story goes that they first struck up an acquaintance on the polo grounds. Camilla simply went up to the Prince, complimented his fine horse and, seizing the moment, flashed Charles a dazzling smile and reminded him that her great-grandmother Alice Keppel had been a close mistress and confidante of his great-grandfather King Edward VII. The Prince immediately sensed in this young lady a kindred spirit and allowed their relationship to develop further. Later, within the royal circle, the possibility of Charles marrying Camilla was discussed. However, the Queen Mother, whose opinion Charles always heeded, categorically struck down Camilla's candidacy: a young lady who had already been involved with other men before marriage, is not fit to be queen someday!

After a while, the lively and cheerful Camilla felt her relationship with the Prince had no future and came to prefer a more acceptable and reliable option: marriage to an officer named Andrew Parker Bowles. Charles was crushed. He had not expected their parting to be so painful.

Meanwhile, another English aristocratic family saw its own drama unfold, as a result, the marriage of the Viscount Althorp and his wife fell apart, and their four children were split into two hostile camps on their mother and father's side, respectively. Little Diana, Charles's future bride, was one of these children. Since the Viscountess was convicted of adultery, the father was given custody of the children, but Viscount Althorp fell into such a deep depression that he was unable to give the little ones enough attention and care.

Subsequently, Diana's childhood was just as sad as the crown prince's. She displayed no especial academic success, but from an early age she showed a gift for caring for those in need. After finishing school and awaiting a suitable match, Diana – a rich and eligible bride – found a job that truly appealed to her: working in a kindergarten. Diana had no doubt that an equally rich and eligible bachelor awaited her, and she even told her loved ones that her wedding would surely be held in Westminster Abbey, the traditional marriage venue of royals.

With regard to Charles and Camilla, they soon rekindled their relationship, and now she became his favourite, in spite of being the wife of an officer. This affair between the bachelor Prince and a married lady and mother of two children, dragged on for several years. There was unease at Buckingham Palace, for the years were slipping by, but the heir to the throne had put no thought into finding a suitable bride. The press periodically reported on his romances with other girls, but none of these involvements ever suggested wedding bells. The subsequent downturn in the British economy saw a decline in the monarchy's popularity.

Throughout the kingdom rumours circulated about a long-running affair between the Prince of Wales and a married lady. Everyone knows how the similar story involving Charles' forebear had ended: Edward VIII abdicated because the royal family would not accept a divorcee. To stave off a crisis, those close to the Prince reminded him that he needed to finally choose a woman and marry, for the sake of maintaining the monarchy's authority.

Thus, the Queen's longing to see her son married and Diana's dreams of marrying a real prince came together. At a social gathering the press noticed that Charles was paying the young Lady Spenser a great deal of attention. The young lady was also making an effort to ingratiate herself with him, she noticed his mournful nature and expressed her desire to support him. The thirty-year-old bachelor was touched. A courtship began. Nevertheless, as it became clear later, Charles did not stop seeing the married Camilla. The royal family agreed with the Prince's choice and nudged him to marry her in every way they could. The crown prince liked Diana, but she lacked the ease, complete dedication, and immediate understanding of his moods and needs that his long-time lover had, and so the Prince hesitated. Charles' parents intervened and reminded him that the young lady was still young and innocent, and if Charles courted her without a marriage ever following, it could compromise her chances. Charles had to either stop seeing her completely, or make it official with an engagement and marriage.

After a lengthy indecision, the heir to the British crown made his choice and proposed marriage to Lady Diana; she immediately accepted. The fact that the two of them had very little in common soon became clear. Charles liked rural life, gardening and hunting with hounds. Diana preferred to stay in the city. Charles loved to listen to classical music, Diana preferred rock. The saddest thing about it all is that, once married, they no longer enjoyed communicating with each other, they no longer tried to agree on anything and they even competed with one other to get the most sympathy from the press.

To this union, doomed almost from the very start, Prince William (second in line to the throne) and Prince Harry were born. But even the birth of two fine sons could not save the marriage. The press relished the chance to report all the scandalous details. Diana, hurt by her husband's infidelity, no longer accepted any prohibitions on what she could and could not do. The public's sympathy unquestionably lay with her. Society's interest in whatever speeches Charles might give on improving the UK was significantly less than the rapt attention given to the charming Diana as she hastened to assist the suffering, brought up the young princes, and alas, suffered her husband's affair with another woman.

Among Diana's major merits in the public's eye, was her dedication to peace making. One particular photograph of Diana became known around the world: clad in a protective suit, she walked through an Angolan minefield with mine-removal experts and thus risked her own life, all for the sake of raising the awareness of this problem. The French

Parliament even suggested that, in recognition of Diana's services, the international treaty banning landmines be named after her.[25] Currently, the Ottawa Treaty banning land mines has been signed by one hundred and thirty-three nations. One notices that among the countries which have *not* ratified the treaty are three members of the UN Security Council: China, Russia and the United States.

And so, in the wake of long-running domestic disagreements, in 1992, the couple announced that they would now be maintaining separate homes. Charles went to live at Clarence House, a home belonging to his grandmother, the Queen Mother. Several years later, the Prince and Princess of Wales officially divorced. Diana kept her title Princess of Wales, but she was stripped of the privilege of being called Her Royal Majesty. It is said that in response, Prince William, the heir to the British throne after Charles, promised to return to his mother her full title when he became king. No one then could have ever imagined that the worst in Charles and Diana's drama was yet to come.

The troubled marriage of many years between Camilla and her husband Andrew Parker Bowles also came to an end. The path to marrying the Prince of Wales was now open to Camilla.

Ever since the moment when the general public became aware of problems in Prince Charles and Diana's marriage, the public has tried to cast blame on one side or the other. It was the royal family itself who had wanted to welcome Diana among their fold, and Diana did try the best she could to live up to her new role as a member of such an august family. She bore healthy and handsome heirs, and she spent a great deal of time on bringing them up, as well as on charitable endeavours. She managed to win true love from her fellow countrymen and global society. Where was there any mistake in that?

It is possible that the Princess of Wales did not conform to the responsibility of being an unshakable public persona who could appropriately merge into the royal ranks and bear everything silently. That is, only superficially, did Diana seem a suitable candidate for the role of the wife of the future king: her lovely appearance, her innocence, her ability to attract the interest and sympathy of the masses. But when the royal family gave Diana such an important place in their corporation, they missed clear signs that the young lady had an extremely vulnerable and unstable personality, psychological traumas that had been inflicted on her in childhood, and she lacked a high degree of education and erudi-

---

25   Viktor Israelyan, *Diplomatiya – moya zhizn'* (MBA, 2006), p. 193.

tion (which also leaves its mark on a person's intellect and the solutions they choose to the problems that arise).

Perhaps under circumstances that were favourable, these qualities of Diana's would never have been an issue. But this was not the case with Charles, who, in everything, was thinking about his love for the more mature, lively and confident Camilla.

On 31 August 1997, a car carrying Diana and her boyfriend Dodi Fayed, while attempting to evade the paparazzi, crashed at full speed into a pillar in a Paris tunnel. The Princess of Wales died in the crash. In 2005, the thirty-five-year-long romance of Charles and Camilla was made official with marriage. The current spouse of the future king bears the title of Duchess of Cornwall.

The royals leave their trace in Russia (1990–2002)

Princess Anne
visits Volgograd (1990)

In 1990, the USSR Ministry of Foreign Affairs notified the Volgograd municipal administration that in June, Her Royal Majesty Princess Anne would be coming to the country on an official visit. The Princess expressed her desire to visit, among other cities, Volgograd, so famous for its victory in the Battle of Stalingrad and recognized in 1943, by her grandfather King George VI, with his gift of a sword of honour.

Here, we will discuss in greater detail the life of Princess Anne, the Queen Mother's granddaughter. Anne is the second child (after Prince Charles) of Queen Elizabeth II and the Duke of Edinburgh. She was born on 15 August 1950 at Clarence House in London. As a child, Anne was very different from her elder brother; she was very active and sporty. From early childhood she loved equestrianism. It can be assumed that in Anne's lifestyle, her mother, Elizabeth II, realized her dream of simple country living: caring for children, horses and other darlings.

The Princess sat astride her first pony at the age of two and a half, and it was her mother, the Queen, who introduced Anne to riding at that time. The Princess learned not only to ride on horseback but also to care for these animals: to remove their saddles for the night, feed them, give them water, brush them and wrap their legs. In paying so much attention to horses, Anne made equestrianism a major part of her own life. Thus, her childhood fascination with horses turned into a sporting career. Princess Anne became the first member of the royal family to win a title at an international sporting event. In 1971, she became European champion in eventing. In 1973, she competed in the same tournament in Kyiv, and, in 1976, at the Montreal Olympics. Her Royal Majesty has also taken part in many competitions in her own country.

Princess Anne's first marriage with Captain Mark Phillips can also be traced back to a gathering for horse enthusiasts. The two young people were joined by a common love for equestrianism, and their romance eventually led to a plush royal wedding. The photographs of the happy Princess in her bridal gown and her handsome groom were shown around the world.

Like something out of a thriller novel was a mentally ill man's attempt to kidnap the Princess just a few months after her wedding. During the attack, the Princess's bodyguard was seriously wounded, and later he was awarded the George Cross for bravery. Anne herself showed enviable calm and composure, refusing to step out of the car and surrender to the attacker, even as he had his gun pointed at her. The Princess was celebrated in the press for such courage.

I shall mention one other prominent quality of Princess Anne. It is well known that Her Royal Majesty has little tolerance for photojournalists. Once she said to one who was especially tiresome and persistent in his attempt to get a shot, "How much are they going to pay you for the photo of me in the bath that you are so insistent on?" The paparazzo named a sum (and it was a considerable one). "Alright," the Princess replied. "Take your photo, then, and we'll split the money between us!"

The Princess's first marriage with a commoner resulted in two children, Peter and Zara. Sadly, this union of two people passionate about horses did not last, and as they ended their sporting careers their marriage declined. In 1992, the spouses divorced by mutual agreement.

Let me add a romantic stroke to the portrait of the stern Princess. Soon after the divorce, Her Royal Majesty married again, out of ardent love. Earlier, the letters from her paramour Timothy Laurence had been stolen and handed over to the press, but Buckingham Palace swiftly bought them after recognizing that they were personal. Elizabeth II gave her consent to her daughter Anne's marriage with this new man and thus recognized its legitimacy. With regard to the Queen Mother, she found a good pretext to avoid being present at her granddaughter's second wedding. The press subsequently saw the Queen Mother's act as a sign that the august lady felt that marriage is something inviolable, and she did not want to be part of anything that might undermine the institution of marriage.

In reality, these second marriages among members of the royal family have not weakened the institution of marriage so much in relation to the authority that the monarchy holds. If we recall how the Duke of Windsor and the divorcee Wallis Simpson were ousted from the family, the Queen Mother could not contradict herself and bless the second marriage of her granddaughter.

Let us return, however, to 1990 and the eve of Her Royal Majesty Princess Anne's visit to the USSR. At the time, Volgograd's chief authority was Yury Starovaty, in his role as chairman of the municipal Council of People's Deputies. He had often met with British visitors before, who had come mainly from Volgograd's twin city Coventry. Now, however, the municipal administration began preparations to welcome a member of the royal family. A route was planned that would take Princess Anne across Volgograd. The details of this royal visit, I owe to two people who personally welcomed Her Royal Majesty: Yury Starovaty and Yury Chekhov (mayor of Volgograd 1991–2003).

The Princess's visit was held with all pomp and ceremony, and was a major event in the city on the Volga. Anne arrived on a small but, by Russian standards, dashing British plane and the Volgograd delegation welcomed her at the airport. She was accompanied by her own retinue of guards in red uniforms and huge fur hats. According to eye witness' accounts, her own clothing was simple but elegant.

Though Princess Anne was a rather reticent person, Yury Starovaty, who was once a bicycle racer of note, quickly established a good rapport with this lady who was known for her equestrian achievements. In their conversation, Starovaty mentioned the work of the Olympic Committee. This was a subject close to both of their hearts, for in 1983 the Princess was honorary president of the British Olympic Association and in 1988 she served on the International Olympic Committee. Moreover, in 1986 she had been named president of the International Federation for Equestrian Sports. Thus, her thoughts on organizing sport were valued.

In accordance with the route traditionally planned for high-ranking visitors, Her Royal Majesty visited the city's famous tractor plant, where she was given a model tractor as a gift. The Princess herself, mentioned that at her country estate she had a real tractor of her own, which she had learned to drive for her own plant-growing needs.

Another item presented to Princess Anne was a huge metal statuette, a replica of the *The Motherland Calls* monument. This was a gift from the mayor. An amusing situation ensued when the British pilot worried that the plane would be unable to take off with such a heavy cargo of gifts.

At the Battle of Stalingrad Museum, Princess Anne held the sword which King George VI had ordered to be made for the heroic city, and she left as a gift to the museum, a photograph of George where he stands on a Buckingham Palace balcony reviewing a parade on Victory Day.

During the dinner in honour of this esteemed guest's visit, the Princess was offered, among other dishes, sturgeon caviar. The Princess ate little, however, and preferred to drink pineapple juice.

On the following day, Her Royal Majesty visited the famous Volga hydroelectric station. She was impressed by its enormity and then, in accordance with her planned schedule, flew to Kyiv. Before saying farewell, the Princess gave Yury Starovaty the gift of her portrait in a royal frame decorated with her initials.

I have had the opportunity to see this photograph where the Princess is looking, with utter composure, directly at the camera. On the fine metal frame, the Princess's first initial "A" is engraved atop and it is also adorned with a crown. The mayor to whom this gift was presented, explained that this portrait which he received from a member of the royal family serves as a sign of a special favour.

However, for this visit the Princess had warned in advance that she does not care for journalists and she asked that there would be no photographers present. Nevertheless, a black-and-white photo was taken of Anne during her visit to the Battle of Stalingrad Museum and it is now held in the museum.

In early 1990, the Princess published her memoirs of her life with horses, and in this book she looks back to her visit to Kyiv many years before. The Soviet Union had not made a good impression on her at the time, and her observations are entirely fair. For example, Anne was troubled to find that the Russian athletes had worse living conditions than the others, and they were forbidden from interacting with their foreign counterparts. Also a black mark on the country, were the empty shop shelves, the long queues and the exceptionally poor service.

Having visited Russia herself, the Princess probably followed, with interest, the changes that occurred there. Nothing is known of any critical remarks made regarding her Volgograd visit. With regard to the Princess's feelings about the present book, she supported the writing of it and kindly sent me a photo of herself, with permission to use it in my book.

Ground laid for a visit from the Queen: Her Majesty in Russia (1994)

The Russian side had previously taken the initiative to establish contacts with the British royal family. Initially, as you will recall, there could be no question of such ties, due to the Soviet regime's murder of the Romanovs, close relatives of the Windsors.

Decades later, it was Margaret Thatcher who vetoed a visit by Elizabeth II to Moscow. The Iron Lady, who recognized what resonance such a visit might have, recommended that this trump card be played at some later moment, which she thought more appropriate. But eleven years on, Thatcher's unprecedented reign in what had hitherto been an exclusively male bastion of power, came to an end and the Prime Minister was forced to retire. Now the matter of contacts between the Russian government and the British crown would be decided by the next Prime Minister.

In 1991, the new British Prime Minister, John Major, visited Moscow, and subsequently the UK readily recognized Russia as the successor of the USSR, and launched a program to deepen ties and actively support the reforms being carried out in Russia. The first Russian president was invited to London and there a partnership between the two countries was signed.

In 1992, the first Russian President and the British Queen met for the first time. Boris Yeltsin invited Her Majesty to visit Moscow at any time she found convenient. This offer was taken up, and the official visit of the Queen to Russia was set for November 1994.

For the British monarchy, experts claim, the early 1990s were one of the most turbulent periods in history. The reason for this was the loud criticism of the monarchy by the Commonwealth nations, and the three failed marriages of the Queen's children: Prince Charles and Diana, Prince Andrew and Sarah and Princess Anne and Mark. A brutal fire in Windsor Castle, where Elizabeth II spent her childhood, added to this gloomy picture. To top it all, in 1993 Her Majesty was compelled to start paying taxes on her income, just like all her subjects do.

An appropriate moment was chosen for the royal visit to Russia. The hope was that the unique nature of this journey, and the establishment of firmer bilateral contacts would bring the monarchy some good news coverage to offset the succession of gloomy stories. The British ambassador to Moscow arranged a preliminary press conference during which he explained to the local journalists, still unfamiliar with the Queen, that Her Majesty does not give interviews and she was to be contacted strictly through official channels.

Thus, on 17 November 1994, Her Majesty Queen Elizabeth II arrived in Russia on a special flight. She was accompanied by her husband the Duke of Edinburgh. It must be mentioned that at this stage, due to the huge changes taking place in Russia, most Russians were entirely focused on their own domestic problems. Therefore, the Queen's visit was of greater interest to the Russian government and representatives of the media than to the Russian population.

What did this famous royal visit consist of? As journalists had been notified beforehand, there would be no signing of important documents between the two parties, but nevertheless, the visit did have political significance. The Queen's schedule during her visit was packed.

The Queen settled in, as befits a member of the royal family, at the Kremlin, the luxury and antiquity of which deeply impressed her. Together, with President Yeltsin and his wife, the royal couple visited the Bolshoi Theatre to see a performance of the ballet *Giselle*. One wonders whose idea it was to show the royals this particular ballet. The staged plot of a worried prince in love with a commoner probably led Elizabeth to muse on similar problems with another prince, her son Charles. Among other events during the visit, an especially important moment came when Her Majesty laid a wreath on the tomb of the Unknown Soldier; the walkway leading up to it lists Russia's heroic cities and among them glorious Stalingrad. (Just a few years later, in 2000, that city on the Volga would become part of the Windsor dynasty's history.) For the royal couple, paying their respects at the war memorial was especially significant, as they had both served in World War II. The Duke of Edinburgh was especially proud of his contribution to our common victory.

As the head of the Church of England, Elizabeth II has shown great interest in religion and its meaning for Russia. It is well known that Her Majesty is a deeply devout person, she never misses a Sunday service and she keeps the fast – during a visit to Rome in her youth she was extremely surprised that many inhabitants of this capital city of Catholicism do not observe Lent. A significant meeting was held between the Queen and Patriarch Alexei II, head of the Russian Orthodox Church, and she visited Uspensky Cathedral. As an Anglican and the Defender of the Faith, she expressed her wish to visit St Andrew's, the Protestant church in Moscow, founded in 1825. By visiting, the Queen literally brought this church back to life, because after the establishment of the Soviet regime it had been shut down like other independent churches. Only upon the Queen's visit did President Yeltsin issue a special decree to hand St Andrew's back over to the Anglican mission, which could not have failed to please Her Majesty. This step also strengthened bilateral ties between the two countries.

Her Majesty also unveiled a memorial plaque marking the renovation of Moscow's English Court, which Ivan the Terrible had granted to English traders in order to spur trade between the two nations. In 1556, the Russian Tsar donated this old palatial building next to Red Square, to English diplomats and traders. It was specially restored in 1994 for the visit of Queen Elizabeth II.

Years later, I was thrilled to follow, myself, in the footsteps of the Queen, to discover what had been preserved in Moscow's English Court many ago and to imagine what all this was like centuries before. The old stone building on Varvarka Street is easily recognizable from afar, due to its Gothic spire. Inside the building are several rooms in the old style, and also a narrow winding staircase leading visitors upwards, which my curiosity led me to follow to the second floor, though the stone steps were very steep. When I came back down the staircase, wearing high heels, I lost my footing slightly and this experience convinced me that ascending was probably safer than descending. In the rooms of the building everything smelled old, the interiors had been kept in a style evoking the classic Soviet film *31 June*. One room featured a long table made from dark wood and was surrounded by high and heavy chairs that had been elaborately carved. I was especially impressed by the beautiful English fireplaces.

The Queen has focused her work especially on matters of culture and education, and therefore, the packed schedule of her tour of Moscow included a visit to Moscow Public School No. 20, where Her Majesty had the opportunity to observe approaches to teaching in Russia and to speak directly with schoolchildren. One can imagine how interesting this must have been to her as a mother of four children.

Traditionally, the exact details of all audiences with the British monarch are kept confidential, and one can only guess at what the Russian President and Elizabeth II must have talked about. From statements which came out later, we know that both sides expressed their satisfaction with the growing ties between their countries and noted areas for future cooperation. As the British monarch is not directly engaged in politics, these two heads of state did not make any specific promises to one another.

Among the curious features of this eminent visit was the excessive care taken by the police, who had the Kremlin cleared of visitors. Her Majesty had been counting on meeting ordinary Russian citizens, and not just members of the government. We can recall her mother's fearlessness in going out among the masses during her own official visits. Elizabeth II inherited that same way of interacting with the people.

The importance of this royal visit is underscored by the fact that the Russian side took concrete actions to meet certain British interests: the restoration of St Andrew's Anglican Church in Moscow, the memorial plaque for the renovation of the English Court in the city centre and definitive solutions to some long-running problems with the new British embassy building. It was the Queen who laid a memorial stone at the site of the new embassy's building on Sofiyskaya Naberezhnaya. In Saint-Petersburg, an embankment which had been renamed after the Red Navy was restored to its former name of the English Embankment.

Let me also mention a humorous side of this serious royal visit. In Saint-Petersburg, during a royal reception on board Her Majesty's yacht *Britannia*, something amusing happened. Because the organizers had not provided complete information when announcing this event, they had not specified that black tie was required; all the invited male guests came wearing ordinary suits as seemed appropriate. But one high official did arrive in a tuxedo, and when he saw that the other guests in their suits were looking at him oddly, he felt like the veritable black sheep and rushed to find a place where he could change into something else. According to my source, he had to change his clothes in his car.

To end my description of this politically significant visit to Russia by the Queen, I shall mention something about the transportation which she used during her travels. Her Majesty arrived in Moscow on a special flight, in Moscow she moved about in her own Rolls-Royce, specially brought from England, and she left Russia by taking the royal yacht *Britannia*, from Saint-Petersburg.

A Soviet memorial from Volgograd erected in London (1999)

Both sides – that is, both the visitors and those who welcomed them – were pleased with the results of the first royal visit to Russia. During the royal couple's stay in Moscow and Saint-Petersburg, the ground was laid for expanding bilateral ties between Russia and the UK, and consequently, outside London's Imperial War Museum, it became possible to erect a memorial to the twenty-seven million Soviet citizens who perished in World War II. Furthermore, the Queen Mother could now be made an honorary citizen of Volgograd. The changed situation, the atmosphere and these more firmly established ties between these two citizens facilitated these contacts.

According to archival material which the Volgograd municipal administration provided to me, during an event in the UK, marking the fiftieth anniversary of the end of World War II, veterans of the Arctic Convoys and the Society for Co-operation in Russian and Soviet Studies, together with the Imperial War Museum, launched an initiative to erect a memorial in London to the Soviet soldiers who fell in the battle with fascism.

British society showed support for these initiatives, and soon, an organizing committee was set up to create the memorial. The Russian side was represented by the Russian Embassy in the UK and Rossotrudnichestvo. Thus, the memorial became a joint Russian–British project and it was understood that it would be jointly funded. The Russian side was to create the actual sculpture and have it delivered to London. The British side began preparing the plot of land for it, and also took on the responsibility of maintaining the memorial and the land around it in the future.

The Russian embassy and Rossotrudnichestvo, undertook the task of raising funds to bring this project to life. Vladimir Molchanov, the embassy's First Secretary, oversaw these efforts, and through the discussions he carried out, the Russian National Bank elected to pay for the memorial. As for the English side, their costs were calculated at twenty thousand pounds sterling, which was raised through donations.

Meanwhile, among the proposals submitted to a competition, British society showed the greatest interest in a work by Volgograd sculptor Sergei Shcherbakov, which most readily expressed the idea behind the memorial. According to the intentions of this memorial, it should aim to remind future generations of the past without any ideological bias regarding the war. Moreover, it was important to take into account Britain's traditions of monumental sculpture and fit with the surrounding architecture and landscape.

Sergei Shcherbakov's sculpture of a grieving woman met these requirements and was used for the memorial. When I spoke with the acclaimed sculptor, I asked him how his work differed from the other works presented in the competition. To understand his reply, we should look once more at his creation. The image of a grieving woman recalls a chapel, doesn't it? The sculptor intended the bell held in the woman's raised hands – a bell that lacks a ringer – to represent grief in an endless minute of silence. Of all the designs submitted, his monument, standing at the crossroads of sculpture and architecture, serves as an invitation to remember, while also being free of any partisan references to the war, and it also fits in with the surrounding space. Shcherbakov's work requires no translation or explication. Everyone understands what this grieving woman is meant to evoke.

In spite of the political disputes that arose in 1999 between Russia and the UK after NATO's bombing of Yugoslavia, the Soviet memorial was unveiled outside the Imperial War Museum on the appointed day.

As Russian Ambassador Yury Fokin explained:

> It had originally been planned that Igor Ivanov, as Minister of Foreign Affairs, would give a speech, but the circumstances arising in connection with Yugoslavia did not allow him to leave Moscow. In short, I was instructed to unveil the memorial. It was a fine ceremony and many people attended, including representatives of a number of former Soviet countries. British veterans took part and veterans' organizations were well represented. The British side brought the Duke of Kent (a cousin of Queen Elizabeth II). As I learned from a conversation with the Queen Mother, she had been kept updated about this upcom-

ing event, and the Duke of Kent later told her about what had taken place.

The highest authorities of various countries sent telegrams acknowledging the unveiling of the memorial. The British newspaper *The Times*, reported on a small protest by Londoners against the bombing of Belgrade that spontaneously broke out during the event.

It is noteworthy that during the unveiling of the memorial, a time capsule from various heroic cities, Volgograd included, was placed at the base of the monument. Inside the capsule is a letter to our descendants about the horrendous twentieth-century catastrophe that was World War II, how many millions of lives it cost and how this memorial represents people's wish to end war and step forward into the twenty-first century, hand in hand and in a unanimous desire to live in peace and prosperity.

When I spoke with Shcherbakov, I learned that his idea of sculpting this grieving woman had arisen long before this British competition in the late 1990s. What led him to conceive of it? It was the historical heritage of his native city which had constantly reminded him of its trials and tribulations since his early childhood.

In spite of the sculptor's youth, he already had a number of prestigious projects behind him by the time he took part in the British competition. A copy of the same grieving-woman sculpture that resides in London had been erected in Shcherbakov's own country in 1997, namely near Volgograd at the Soviet military cemetery in Rossoshki. There are some differences between the Russian and British versions of the sculpture. The height of the Rossoshki monument is 7.60 metres, while in London it stands at 3.60 metres tall. The Russian grieving woman is made from concrete and forged copper, while its British sister sculpture is cast from bronze. According to the sculptor, he made corresponding changes in the proportions of his second version.

It is hard to overstate the significance of this Russian memorial's unveiling in London. During the Cold War, the two countries did not appreciate the scale of the sacrifice that the other side had made for the sake of our common victory. Now the Soviet memorial in London stands as an eternal testimony to the contribution which twenty-seven million victims made to freedom from fascism. In accordance with tradition, thrice yearly, those who feel it important to honour the memory of the Soviet defenders gather at the monument: 9 May on Victory Day, 27 January on International Holocaust Remembrance Day and in mid

November on the British Memorial Sunday. Veterans of the Arctic Convoys and leaders and ambassadors of former Soviet countries, visit the memorial during their trips to London. Here, they solemnly commemorate their compatriots who laid down their lives for this victory.

In June 2003, President Vladimir Putin visited this unique London memorial. The Russian President was then on a state visit to the UK, having accepted an invitation from Queen Elizabeth. This visit was of special significance, considering that the last such high-ranking visit in these countries' history had happened one hundred and thirty years ago.

In conclusion, let me refer to the remarks made by Jean Turner, Secretary of the Soviet Memorial Trust Fund, at the unveiling of the monument. This memorial, she said, was created in a spirit of peace and reconciliation, and it aims to communicate what suffering war can bring, and how vital is to maintain harmony between peoples.

An English Queen and Stalingrad

Now I shall come to the main topic for which this book was written. As mentioned above, when I studied the large number of biographies written about the Windsor dynasty, I found almost no mention of what links Volgograd and the august royal family of Britain.

Only in the lushly illustrated *Her Majesty Queen Elizabeth The Queen Mother* by Margaret Irene Laing and James Bishop, did I find a brief note that on 12 April 2000, the Queen Mother was named an honorary citizen of Volgograd.

However, at the dawn of the new millennium, Volgograd's granting of honorary citizenship to the Queen Mother had enormous resonance across the world, and it sparked in Volgograd's inhabitants, a desire to learn as much as they could about the royals.

When I began to study the life of the Queen Mother, I was primarily interested in what connects Her Majesty to Volgograd. In response, official organizations in the city on the Volga told me about the city's ties with its twin city, Coventry, about the visit Clementine Churchill had made and about the help which ordinary British people provided during World War II (which truly played an important role in establishing ties between the two countries). When it came to members of the royal family themselves, here, the only thing mentioned was the King's sword held at the Battle of Stalingrad Museum or newspaper articles about humanitarian missions. There was not a single document about help being given personally by the Queen Mother. In fact, one might have doubted whether such assistance had been rendered at all. I was interested in whether there might be any documents proving that the monarchy personally contributed material assistance to help Russia in general and Stalingrad in particular.

As I studied the life of the Queen Mother as set out in the British royal encyclopaedia (information on this was sent to me by the royal archives at Windsor Castle), I noted that during World War II, Her Majesty had been president of the British Red Cross. I had already seen mentions of this organization somewhere before.

There is proof! In Clementine Churchill's book *My Visit to Russia* (of which a Russian translation is held at the Battle of Stalingrad Museum), the author explains that the Aid to Russia Fund was founded in the autumn of 1941 under the British Red Cross. It was to the Red Cross that I directed my next request for information on what assistance the Queen might have provided.

And here is what I received in response from the British Red Cross's archives. Museum employee Emily Oldfield, told me that while she studied the materials in the archives dating to that time, she found a mention of the humanitarian assistance provided by the royal family during the war years. When the committee for assisting Russia met for the first time on 21 October 1941, the minutes of the meeting state that the King and Queen donated three thousand pounds sterling to a Red Cross assistance fund which the Duke of Gloucester (the King's younger brother) had set up. Moreover, it was recorded that they decreed that one thousand pounds sterling go to the Aid to Russia Fund led by Clementine Churchill. We then find a detailed calculation of the donation: seven hundred and fifty pounds sterling from the King and two hundred and fifty pounds sterling from the Queen. In addition, this document states that the dowager, Queen Mary, had made a donation of two hundred pounds sterling to the Aid to Russia Fund. The total from the royal family was one thousand two hundred pounds sterling.

The mystery does not end here, however. The King, along with his wife and the widowed Queen Mary, strangely vanished from the official list of those who had donated to assist Russia (in these papers, many other famous names are shown to have donated, Clementine Churchill included, who provided a cheque for one hundred pounds sterling). I again turned to Emily Oldfield, the Red Cross museum employee responsible for the archives, for an explanation. I asked her to see whether the names of the royal couple appeared in subsequent lists of contributors. Her response was: their names are not recorded. But this does not mean that they never donated. Vital evidence that the royals did make a donation is the initial royal decree that their money go to the Aid to Russia Fund. Therefore, the search for documentation in England had to go on.

For further proof of their involvement, let us turn now to the volume "The Grand Alliance" of Winston Churchill's memoir *The Second World War*, more specifically, the passage describing Clementine Churchill's first call for humanitarian aid to Russia. Winston Churchill recounts a conversation with his wife, where he explained to her why immediate military assistance to Russia was not possible. He suggested that at that stage, Russia should be supplied all manner of war materiel, and that funds should be raised for medical assistance. Clementine agreed to head the Aid to Russia campaign and, in late October (the date matches the information provided by the Red Cross: 21 October 1941), Mrs Churchill made her powerful appeal:

> There is no one in this country whose heart has not been deeply stirred by the appalling drama now going on in Russia. […] Our gracious and beloved King and Queen, in sending a further £3000 to the Red Cross last week, expressed a wish that £1000 of their joint gift should be allocated to the Aid to Russia Fund. They have set a characteristic example. […] Thus, from the King and Queen to the humblest wage-earner and cottage-dweller, we can all take part in this message of good-will and compassion. […] There are millions of people who would like to share in this tribute to the Russian people.

Cambridge University holds the most complete archive of Churchill's papers. I asked the archive to help me find the lost document on the royals' personal contribution during World War II. Richard Calver, an employee at the archive, replied that they have not been able to locate any documents relating to the royals' donation. As proof, we only have the mention in Churchill's *The Second World War* which I quoted above, and a reference to a donation in the minutes from the British Red Cross meeting in the autumn of 1941. I had contacted the Windsor Castle archives with the same inquiry back at the beginning of my research. The wording of their answer emphasized that no such papers were found in the archives, but that does not mean that they never existed. It may be that they are held in another location or have been lost entirely.

However, in spite of the incomplete documentation at present, we can take it for granted that a donation of one thousand two hundred pounds, really was made by the royal family and it ultimately arrived, together with other such donations, in Stalingrad and other cities in need of assistance. Through this money, medicines were purchased that were loaded onto the Arctic Convoy ships among other cargo, and then delivered to the USSR.

It was not for any sum of money that Elizabeth was named an honorary citizen of Stalingrad. There had been even larger donations, such as that of Lord Nuffield who sent a cheque for fifty thousand pounds. Her Majesty was awarded honorary citizenship for her distinguished services in arranging assistance from the UK people for Stalingrad during World War II and for her role in the development of friendly ties with Russia.

According to the Battle of Stalingrad Museum, the numerous donations made by Her Majesty's subjects to help rebuild Stalingrad went to such things as restoring a hospital in January 1943, through funds from the Labourist Fund, five portable power plants and four hundred thousand metres of power-distribution lines, as well as a telephone exchange supporting ten thousand phone numbers. In May 1943, a special fund at the National Labour Organization aimed to raise seventy-five thousand pounds to help equip a Stalingrad hospital, but ultimately, it was able to send a cheque for a whole one hundred thousand pounds. The list could go on. The culminating moment of such assistance to Russia was Clementine Churchill's visit to the country on a humanitarian mission for the Aid to Russia Fund under the Red Cross.

At Volgograd's Museum of Health Care History, among other precious exhibits of the visit, a silver teaspoon is held, which has the royal initials of George VI engraved on it – a unique relic of the solidarity that was proclaimed.

Testimony to the help provided in rebuilding the city is provided by various documents, now yellowed by time, as well as in the imperishable symbol of Britain's solidarity with Stalingrad: the sword of honour gifted by King George VI. By 1999, when the idea first arose of naming Her Majesty an honorary citizen of the city, the Queen Mother had, herself, become a symbol of Britain and the assistance rendered to Stalingrad during its World War II hardships.

A continuation of this growing closeness between Russia and the UK, were the preparations to name Queen Mother Elizabeth an honorary citizen of Volgograd.

The idea of awarding the Queen Mother this honorary title first arose in the Russian embassy in London, when the unveiling of the Soviet memorial was being celebrated. These initial discussions involved Ambassador Yury Fokin and members of the Volgograd municipal administration. The deliberations took place in a rather famous room at the embassy, which has come to be known as the "Maisky office", for it was precisely here where Ivan Maisky worked during his years as ambassador (1932–1943). Here is how Yury Fokin describes that moment:

The office is on the first floor and features elegant wood trim. It has still kept the style of that era. I usually do not show visitors to my own office, I always talk with them in the "Maisky office". We did have our suspicions, however, that this office might be susceptible to eavesdropping, as it looks out on a part, albeit small, of the embassy's garden. During that particular discussion it was suggested that the Queen Mother be named an honorary citizen of Volgograd. The idea came from the Volgograders, and it was my pleasure to lend my support to it. The only caveat I expressed was that first one would have to discuss the matter with the Queen Mother's staff. When we first suggested awarding medals to veterans of the Arctic Convoys, it turned out that the British do not have the right to receive honours from foreign countries. When we wanted to award the first medal (I was working in Moscow then on UK issues), I was astonished to learn that the Foreign Office had a strict rule against British citizens receiving honours from foreign states. We later managed to get permission to decorate these veterans. The Queen Mother supported our idea.

Initially, awarding the Queen Mother honorary citizenship of Volgograd was fraught with certain difficulties due to her high rank, which required the greatest delicacy, and also due to the changes in the political situation with regard to Chechnya and the feelings of the UK population. In Volgograd, where, historically, the local population has counted many wartime heroes, each of them feels that it is a great honour to be recognized for their service. The title of honorary citizen of Volgograd can only be awarded to one outstanding individual each year.

In light of the improving relationship with the UK, the Volgograd authorities proposed that they show their gratitude to the Queen Mother, the widow of George VI, under whose reign the city had received such generous aid. After their initiative received the approval of the Russian embassy in London, the Volgograd authorities contacted Her Majesty and requested her consent to receiving the honorary citizenship of the city. The Queen kindly accepted the proposal.

Meanwhile, the local Volgograd media sought to inform the population about the United Kingdom's contribution to their city's restoration, and they reported on what the royal family had done during the war years. On 6 January 2000, the municipal council unanimously passed the resolution, which I quote here:

Having considered the motion of the municipal administration, and taking into account the great contribution which King George VI and his wife Queen Elizabeth made to arranging British assistance for the Soviet Union during World War II, to the development of friendly ties between Russia and the UK, the Volgograd Municipal Council of People's Deputies, in accordance with the Charter of the Heroic City of Volgograd and the Regulation on Honorary Citizenship of Volgograd hereby resolves to award honorary citizenship of Volgograd to Her Majesty Queen Elizabeth (the Queen Mother) and requests her consent to receive this honour, and it resolves also to publish the present resolution in the local media.

The city authorities duly began preparations for the ceremony, in which the Queen would be awarded an honorary diploma and medal. This solemn event was scheduled for April 2000 in London.

13 Kensington Palace Gardens

As I have mentioned several times in this story, the figure of Ambassador Ivan Maisky and events at the Russian embassy in London, I feel it of possible interest to readers to digress and share my own impressions of this important location. I will turn to my diary entries which I made immediately after the events described.

London, 2013… From Rossotrudnichestvo we travel in an embassy car to 13 Kensington Palace Gardens, the residency of the Russian ambassador in London. The white, blue and red of the Russian flag flutters above the home in antique style – a little part of Russia in a foreign country. Today, the ambassador's residence will host a reception for the visit of Russia's Deputy Prime Minister Dmitry Rogozin.

We are back in our own element. As far as I know, this building in Neo-Gothic style dates back to the middle of the nineteenth century. In 1930, its owner, the wealthy businessman Sir Lewis Richardson, gave it to the USSR to use as its embassy. According to the agreement between Russia and the UK, the present annual rent for the building is merely a symbolic figure, one pound sterling. By the same token, the UK pays for its Moscow embassy on Sofiyskaya Naberezhnaya with a merely symbolic rent of one rouble.

The interior of the ambassador's residence has largely been preserved in its old authentic style and it dazzles with its antique furniture and paintings, brought from Moscow, by famous Russian artists: Aivazosky's sea views, the smoky landscapes of Grabar and Kustodiev's canvas *Maslenitsa*.

One of the most magnificent rooms in the embassy, in my opinion, is the orangerie, surrounded by greenery. Inside, it is adorned with huge mirrors in gilded frames and statues extolling female beauty. The orangerie's past is traced through framed photographs hung within. Eminent politicians of ages past, look down on us: here is Winston Churchill and Ambassador Maisky seated at the same table set with crystal glasses and Russian delicacies. The feast shown in this photo took place in this same building. I get the feeling that I am not only coming closer to history, I am also becoming a small part of it myself.

To jump ahead, I will tell of something that I did that I was not aware of myself at that moment. It was here, on the following morning, in this historic orangerie, that I would have a working breakfast with some outstanding diplomats of our time: Russian Ambassador to the UK Alexander Yakovenko, Minister Counsellor Alexander Kramarenko and the diplomatic mission's press secretary A. A. Kozhiny. All of them played a great role in my own understanding of how diplomacy works. One of the results of this morning meeting with these men was a letter from Ambassador Yakovenko to the Governor of the Volgograd Region, which bore a suggestion that the region present to a London audience the opportunities it offered for British investors.

Meanwhile, the large room with a luxurious staircase gradually fills with diplomatic staff. Yes, diplomacy continues to be, with rare exceptions, an all-male bastion. However, with not just a little pride for my fellow Russian woman, I must mention that the world's first female ambassador was Alexandra Kollontai. In her time she was held in very high esteem in the country in which she worked, and she made a significant contribution to the peace settlement between Russia and Finland in 1941.

Also of note is V. I. Popov's opinion of women's contribution. The esteemed authority on the theory and practice of modern diplomacy wrote, "… I knew well the female ambassador of a certain Latin American country in Canberra. We established a close working relationship and I admired that she knew how to obtain serious, valuable information."[26]

I look around and see dapper men in suits and ties, some with gleaming spectacles. They have attentive looks, their manners are restrained and courteous and they speak English. They hold wine glasses in their hands. Among those present, there are ladies as well, some intellectually gifted, while others seem destined to serve as aesthetic decoration for the reception.

It is well known that such events are organized not just for their main official purpose, but also for exchanging valuable information about international political issues. It was all very interesting and intriguing. Around me is a crowd of ladies and I continue my conversation with them. We discuss the London Book Fair which is being held over the

---

26   Viktor Popov, *Sovremennaya diplomatiya* (2003), p. 62.

next few days, the presentation at Rossotrudnichestvo and my book. We consider whether it might be possible to translate it into English for an interested audience.

Then, running somewhat late, the main guest of the event, Dmitry Rogozin, arrives with his entourage. Everyone moves to a room decorated in gold tones, where microphones have already been set up at the lectern, as well as one for the interpreter. Recording equipment too is set up to capture the evening. For the guests, comfortable chairs have been set out.

During the Deputy Prime Minister's speech, he expresses his view that the missile-defence race represents a provocation and a challenge to peace, as it provokes, in turn, an offensive-arms race. His speech is replete with vivid examples and analogies. "Never in the history of mankind has the development of the shield outpaced the development of offensive weaponry," he says. "If someone wants to come up with a better shield, his opponent will definitely come up with a sword with longer and better steel."

The media sum up the Deputy Prime Minister's speech by quoting his statements "One cannot shoot down a bullet with a bullet" and "Whoever prepares for defence, loses." I caught the glimmer of foreign diplomats' pens around me as they apparently noted down his main points.

In ending his speech, the Deputy Prime Minister suggested that efforts would be focused on space monitoring. Humankind's vulnerability to the universe had been clearly exposed by the Chelyabinsk meteorite, which had slipped through the atmosphere, unnoticed, by the world's tracking systems.

After Rogozin finished, members of the audience went up to Rogozin. I myself, and not without the embassy's blessing, struck up a conversation with the man, thanked him for his insightful remarks and offered him a copy of my book on the bilateral ties between Russia and the UK. The Deputy Prime Minister smiled and promised he would read it.

A Conversation with Ambassador Yury Fokin

One of my most illuminating encounters during the writing of this biography of the Queen Mother was my acquaintance with Ambassador Yury Fokin. Of especial interest for the present book was his personal involvement, representing the embassy, in the preparations for awarding the Queen Mother honorary citizenship of Volgograd in 1999. I think it would be of interest to reproduce here our conversation:

Natalia Kulishenko: Mr Fokin, tell me about your interaction with Her Majesty The Queen Mother, who was awarded honorary citizenship of Volgograd in 2000, in part, through your efforts.

Yury Fokin: I had seen the Queen Mother on a number of occasions, but rarely did I speak with her for long. Once, we conversed when I handed her the *Queen* statuette. I should note that the Queen had thoroughly prepared for this meeting, and the two of us spoke for about twenty minutes. She asked me various questions, I mentioned the Soviet memorial which we had erected in London. She had been kept informed, it was the Duke of Kent who had provided her with updates. There is a photograph of him laying a wreath. He gave a speech and I did as well.

As you can see from this photograph, the Queen is very formally yet elegantly dressed, she wears an exquisite dress and a traditional hat. The Queen Mother was famous for her collection of hats, she owned hundreds of them, each for various occasions. For this meeting with an ambassador she had a new hat ordered in order to show her esteem for our country and for the ambassador himself.

During our conversation, she let it be known that she understood the role which Russia had played in the victory over fascism during World War II, where we and the UK were allies. I also mentioned to her that we are aware of how she refused to be evacuated to Canada, of how she remained in London and after each bombing visited the afflicted areas.

In doing so, she had given a considerable boost to Londoners' morale. It was therefore, no accident that she maintained such good ties with war veterans, especially veterans of the Arctic Convoys.

The two of us had also enjoyed a good conversation in the autumn of 1997. Before that, more precisely on 31 July, I had presented my credentials as ambassador, and shortly thereafter, an event was held at the palace, where she was present too. There I had been introduced to her. When we met again on 31 October 1997 at an event for war veterans, she was also there and, when she caught sight of me, she expressed her desire to speak with me.

N. K.: How did your meeting in London in 1999 with the delegation from Volgograd go?

Y. F.: The Volgograd delegation came down to the embassy. We met and chatted. The meeting took place in the "Maisky office". During that particular discussion it was suggested that the Queen Mother be named an honorary citizen of Volgograd. The idea came from the Volgograders, and it was my pleasure to lend my support to it. The only caveat I expressed was that first, one would have to discuss the matter with the Queen Mother's staff. When we first suggested awarding medals to veterans of the Arctic Convoys, it turned out that the British do not have the right to receive honours from foreign countries.

N. K.: When were Russian medals first awarded to veterans of the Arctic Convoys?

Y. F.: The first time we awarded veterans these medals was in Norway. It was in 1995, the fiftieth anniversary of the victory. We decorated some thirty veterans of the war, Norwegians. One Norwegian had worked for British intelligence, and through his efforts – on the basis of information he provided – seven German cargo ships were sunk that had been transporting men and materiel. He would go out to sea in his little boat and observe enemy cargo ships' movements, then he would relay that information to the right place, and British planes would come and bomb them. Then the British lent him to us, and he started to maintain contact with our embassy in Sweden. It was in Sweden where he met Ambassador Alexandra Kollontai. In April 1995, when we sent out invitations for the event at the embassy on 9 May, his wife called and said that he was too ailing to come. Then I told our military attaché that we would get into the car and go to his home. It was about one hundred kilometres from Oslo. When we arrived at his home, he was deeply touched. We awarded him his medal, the military attaché places it on his chest, but he says, "I know the custom you have." He takes the medal off and says, "Of course you brought a bottle of vodka along." I told him that of course we had, we would not have come empty-handed. He asks if we have glasses, too. It turns out that my driver has a set in the boot of the car. We filled his glass to the very brim, he dropped the medal into the vodka, brought it to his lips, and then asked the military attaché's assistant to drink it for him, as his own health would not allow it. Our man downed the vodka. In short, we spent some time chatting very amiably. He again put the medal on and smiled, he was very happy. In early July his wife called to tell us that he had died. But we had managed to award him that honour nevertheless, we had managed to thank him for his service! He had lost his good health when the Germans found out what was going on and then threw him straight into a prison camp.

N. K.: Does his family still have the medal?

Y. F.: Yes. We do not take our medals back, though some countries do have a tradition that decorations should be returned to the state.

So, in London we organized a very fine event. I also took part in the unveiling of a memorial in Scotland: it was a huge stone, exquisitely carved, and it bears an inscription that in this town in north-western Scotland, the Arctic Convoys had been formed to supply arms, food and uniforms to Murmansk and Arkhangelsk. Quite a lot of men – British and Norwegian – died in the Arctic Convoys. The Germans made efforts to track the convoys, and many British men died in the waters of the Arctic. Later, the veterans told me that they had informed the Queen Mother. The organization was under her aegis in a way. When we unveiled the memorial plaque in the crypt of St Paul's Cathedral, she also came. She walked down the stairs on her own, though already both of her legs had been operated on. She moved very slowly, but on her own two feet.

N. K.: Whose initiative was it to unveil this memorial plaque?

Y. F.: The British. I was invited to give a speech, just as I had when we awarded those medals at the embassy in a solemn ceremony with a banquet. At the embassy, the veterans even sang a couple of songs. It is nice when people are able to relax at these events, especially considering their age and the reason for the gathering. The Queen Mother followed these developments and lent her support to them.

N. K.: When were the first medals awarded to British veterans?

Y. F.: The first time Russia decorated these veterans was on 13 October 1997. We had brought the matter up before, but we found that the British have strict rules with regard to foreign decorations. We contacted the Foreign Office. At the time, our request was handled by Ann

Pringle, who is currently UK ambassador in Moscow. She could only shrug and say, "Those are the rules."

We began an effort behind the scenes. We thus informed the veterans' organizations that we had been met by refusal, and they asked the Queen Mother to intervene. She played, as far as I can judge, her role: the next time we brought up the matter of awarding these decorations, Ann Pringle told me, "Alright, go ahead, but don't make a big fuss." However, word got out, even without us doing anything, through the veterans' organizations. Then at a press conference I was even asked, "Is this really going to happen?" I said that yes, it was, but I did not go into details. We expressed our thanks to the British government that they had made an exception for us in this case. So, it was in 1997 that Russia began to decorate British veterans.

N. K.: Mr Fokin, what is your opinion on the books which your colleague, Ambassador Viktor Popov, has written about the UK?

Y. F.: Viktor Popov has written four books about the UK. Of course, he knew best the British diplomatic corps, life in Buckingham Palace. He wrote those books while at the Diplomatic Academy. We got our own academy in 1974, it was in fact Popov's initiative. He convinced Andrei Gromyko that the Higher Diplomatic School (that was what our training facility was called until 1974) should be raised to the level of an academy. Then Gromyko, after yet another conversation… It happened during a walk around our building in New York, and Viktor Popov was part of a delegation. On Saturday, when Gromyko could get out of New York, he left. He loved long walks, and there was a road there, six hundred and fifty metres long, and he would always go out in a full suit, never in shirtsleeves, and with a hat on. He would walk ten laps, some of his deputies and other employees could not keep up with him, because he insisted on a brisk pace. I recall this now because Viktor Popov, who was talking with Gromyko about this matter, was walking alongside him and literally gasping for breath. Gromyko stopped so that Popov could catch his breath, and he said, "Alright, you've convinced me. Now convince five or six members of the Politburo." The document proposing the foundation of a Diplomatic Academy went to the very top, especially since it was a matter which Andrei Gromyko had shown his personal support for. He was not yet a member of the Politburo then, he only became such in 1977, and in 1974 he was still an ordinary minister. Viktor Popov used a very interesting technique. Under the academy a so-called women's circle was organized, it consisted mainly of the wives of high-ranking

Soviet officials, including the wives of several Politburo members. The circle met, if I'm not mistaken, once a month. There would be talks and concerts, our building at Bolshoi Kozlovsky Street allowed the organization of such events. Basically, Viktor Popov spoke with several Politburo members' wives separately, it was a long story. Then, when he told Andrei Gromyko about this, Gromyko said, "Alright then, you will see that the document is sent to the Central Committee." The document was sent to M. A. Suslov, who was at that time the Secretary of the Central Committee, and he forwarded it to the Politburo for review. When the matter came up for a vote, four or five people said, "Yes, of course!"

N. K.: Thanks to those Politburo members' wives?

Y. F.: It is like what English speakers call "pillow talk". When a wife wants to convince her husband of something, then she can gently bring it up when the tired man lays down to sleep. Perhaps the story is apocryphal, but it has been claimed that Viktor Popov used this very technique. We named our academy library in honour of Viktor. After he passed away, we published a book about him with the title *A Brilliant and Worthy Life*. It has a lot of information about his work in general and his ambassadorial career.

N. K.: In one of his books, Popov said that it is a queen's surroundings which moulds her. Who was part of the Queen Mother's surroundings?

Y. F.: The Queen Mother maintained especially close ties with the military community, I mean veterans, and also with organizations dedicated to environmental matters. These, in turn, often used her name in order to achieve certain results. It was a big job. I know that when we set up our Russian National Centre for Heritage Trusteeship, we looked to the analogous organizations in England, Scotland and Wales for examples. I believe Northern Ireland also has trusts for historical conservation. The Queen Mother paid a great deal of attention to their work. All in all, she enjoyed universal love from the British people, people from various spheres would turn to her. I often heard that she helped people, she interceded with the Queen to ask for various things.

N. K.: The correspondence with the Volgograd municipal administration was carried out with the Queen Mother's private secretary, Alastair (judging from his signature). Did you ever interact with him?

Y. F.: We communicated with him when we wanted to award the *Queen* statuette. He told us that the Queen was ready to receive us. I visited her, accompanied by Vladimir Molchanov.

I would like to emphasize that the main circle around the Queen Mother is her family. Like the other members of that family, she serves as patroness for a large number of organizations. Once, at a reception at the British embassy, we sat next to Princess Anne and I told her that, from what I understood, she had taken on a great many tasks for society. She said that this was true and added that she could not even give an exact count of the number of organizations which have asked to be under her aegis, and she had agreed to. This does not actually involve much practical work, but the correspondence alone is very valuable. By the way, the British have a very developed epistolary culture. I have been told that one of the ambassadors in London, after he had received several letters relating to some matter of business or protocol, did not think it important to answer them. He started to ignore them. But if you receive a letter, you have to answer it. If there are any issues that involve us, then a reply is obligatory. Inversely, when I myself wrote letters, I would always receive a reply. The British have that epistolary culture, and it is considered a mark of a person's etiquette.

N. K.: What do you think about Ambassador Maisky's books?

Y. F.: All ambassadors must know how to write, but Maisky was not just a brilliant diplomat, he was also a person with special literary talents. Recently, my friends at the Academy of Sciences gave me as a present, Maisky's diary in three volumes. Hardly a day went by when he did not jot down at least a few lines. These diary entries fill in our understanding of Soviet–British relations and the personalities of various political figures; we get a particularly clear picture of Winston Churchill. Maisky also got on well with the British royals as a whole and with the family of King George VI in particular. He maintained good ties with the British aristocracy, the military, diplomatic corps and the business world. He was a man of many varied interests, and he did a lot for our country. It is not for nothing that his name is widely known, if not among ordinary Russians, then at least among certain circles.

Honorary citizenship of Volgograd for a British Queen

The ceremony for awarding Queen Mother Elizabeth took place on 12 April 2000, in Clarence House, her London home. For a description of the royal home, I will quote here from the account of Yury Fokin, detailing the events of the year before:

> Yes, it was there where we visited her. It is a relatively small castle and it belongs to the Queen Mother. It is furnished, I would say, in a traditional style with a lot of plush furniture, various knick-knacks like probably all women keep. Or in any event, women who have lived such a long life. We entered through a reception room, where we were met by her assistant and also her security people. We were then led into the Queen Mother's chamber: it was a room of about fifty or sixty square metres. She had it kept very warm and cosy. This was on the first floor, and there were only two floors in all. When you drive up, you see two floors decked with ivy. There is a lot of greenery, a lot of flowers. The building does not look out directly on the busy street, so the noise from the street did not especially trouble her. It is an old-style home, but it has been kept in very fine shape.

Thus, it was the year 2000. A representative from the Russian embassy had informed everyone in advance about the etiquette required when dealing with British royalty: how to bow to the monarch when greeting her, how one should not come too close to the august person, shake her hand or hold her by the elbow. Before the start of the ceremony, when all eyes were on the door through which the Queen would enter, it was actually her little Corgi dog that first came into the room. Only after this pet appeared did Her Majesty walk in.

This is actually a feature of British royal hospitality: in order to remove the tension among the audience, who might be intimidated by a looming meeting with a royal, the royals' little pets would be sent in. The pets would freely move through the crowd of guests, get their share of attention and admiration, and thus do their part to make the guests feel more relaxed.

In this first-floor room, the monarchess was awaited by a crowd including Grigory Karasin and his wife, the Mayor and Vice-Mayor of Volgograd, Her Majesty's aide, an interpreter and representatives of the media. On the video made of the event, Elizabeth appears to be wearing an emerald dress and the venerable lady has no hat on. Around her neck she wears a pearl necklace with three rows, two large earrings stick out from underneath her grey and coiffured hair, and a large bracelet is around her wrist. Next to the Queen on this video, one can see the impressive statuette known as *Queen*, a gift from the sculptor of the Soviet memorial in London, Sergei Shcherbakov.

This solemn event lasted longer than planned. And at the age of one hundred this *grande dame* had maintained her clarity of mind, she told those present of how she had watched a film about Volgograd the night before. The heroic city, she said, had greatly impressed her. She recalled the concern Britain felt during the siege of Stalingrad, the unanimous spirit of the British people to assist Stalingrad and their admiration of its victory.

During the awarding of this honour to the Queen Mother, the venerable lady especially brightened at a collection of children's drawings from Volgograd that were dedicated to her. The schoolchildren had drawn the Queen as they imagined her. She went against protocol and spent much longer with the Volgograd delegation than had originally been planned. Her Majesty looked at these imagined depictions of her with great interest and discussed them with the Volgograd delegation. She got so carried away with them that the ambassador postponed his initial plan to talk about other matters with her.

The meeting lasted around forty minutes. The press was provided with the official text which the Volgograd mayor had addressed to the Queen Mother:

Your Majesty:

Today I, the Mayor of the Heroic City of Volgograd, have been asked by the Volgograd City Council to perform the pleasant and honourable task of awarding Your Majesty our city's highest mark of distinction: a medal and diploma, along with the title Honorary Citizen of Volgograd.

This award is given to citizens of Russia and other countries who have rendered outstanding services to our city and whose political and social activities have been recognized by the people of Volgograd.

As we observe the fifty-fifth anniversary of the victory over German fascism, in the battle against which our soldiers shed blood together, the help which the British people provided to our citizens during the war years is a more prominent theme than ever. The first congratulations of our victory and the first assistance given to us came from the British people.

Held in our municipal museum, like the most precious relics, are the gifts from British cities and the sword of honour given by King George VI, as a recognition of the bravery and heroism which Stalingraders showed in the fight with the Nazi invaders. The people of Stalingrad are grateful to you, Your Majesty, and will always cherish the memory of your nation's contribution to Stalingrad's restoration.

We are also grateful to you for the launching of the twin cities movement, for the first twinned cities were Stalingrad and Coventry.

We must especially acknowledge Your Majesty for the May 1999 unveiling in London, of a memorial to the Soviet soldiers and civilians who perished in World War II. This humane and Christian act is worthily revered in Russia, for those who forget the fallen cannot truly appreciate the living. The people of Volgograd have been overjoyed and grateful, Your Majesty, to hear of your consent to our awarding the title Honorary Citizen of Volgograd.

I humbly ask Your Majesty to accept the medal of Honorary Citizen of Volgograd as a symbol of the Volgograd people's recognition of the services which you, the royal family and the entire

British people have rendered in helping to restore Stalingrad, and to strengthen peace and friendship among the peoples of the world.

Your Majesty has been a vital figure for the world, as you have worked for peace all your life long, just like our heroic city of Volgograd which has been recognized by the United Nations as a Messenger of Peace. Now you, Your Majesty, are an honorary citizen of this city. Please allow us, Your Majesty, to wish you good health, and to wish your people prosperity.

I humbly ask Your Majesty to accept the medal and diploma of an Honorary Citizen of Volgograd.

This event had enormous resonance around the world. Major television networks subsequently broadcast the event, and it was also covered in newspapers and magazines. The words of Volgograd's mayor on the recognition of these historical deeds were reproduced: "The British people did much for our city in the time of hardships, in 1943. In the years since we have not forgotten the hospital which Britain equipped for us, nor the telephone switchboard supporting ten thousand numbers which they delivered to us."

The elder Elizabeth was the first foreign person to be named an honorary citizen of the city on the Volga. The Queen Mother's press secretary let it be known that Her Majesty, who had been offered so many titles and honours in her life, had been pleased to accept the honorary citizenship of Volgograd.

One curious fact relates to the Queen Mother's outfit during the award ceremony. Her Majesty appeared in view of the press without her celebrated hat. This may be due to the protocol appropriate for an indoor event as opposed to an outdoor one. Later, one Volgograd newspaper commented on this fact as a mark of the Queen Mother's special favour to the delegation from the former Stalingrad. Views in the UK have differed on whether a royal should wear a hat during a public appearance. One of the tailors to Queen Elizabeth II has said, "When the Queen enters a room, that is a big event. Therefore, she must be wearing a hat out of politeness to her audience."

Yet, even official representatives of Buckingham Palace can be mistaken. For example, in 1953, as Elizabeth II went on her coronation tour of Scotland, a solemn ceremony was held to bless her crown, sceptre and sword. On the advice of her private secretary, the Queen wore an everyday dress to emphasize her democratic values to her Scottish subjects. However, her Scottish subjects had grown used to some pomp in this ancient ritual and they did not appreciate her new twist on it, which in their opinion, suggested a lack of respect for these sacred relics.

The monarchess's last journey, as she wished it

In every era, royal funerals have been events of great historical importance. In the past, the rite of entrusting a deceased monarch's body to the earth has taken place in an atmosphere of strict secrecy and only at night. Queen Victoria was the first to break this tradition; before her death she had issued her own instructions for her burial. Since that time, the modern way of doing things has been called a "Victorian funeral".

Queen Mother Elizabeth, who was never bored in life, also had a philosophical way of relating to death. For many years she had already planned her own funeral down to the smallest details. This included such things as the music to accompany the ceremony (Beethoven's funeral march), the places which the procession was to pass (Clarence House and Buckingham Palace, among others), and the fact that the flowers from her grave were to be laid at the tomb of the Unknown Soldier.

One might have expected this Scottish-born woman of royal blood, who had enjoyed such a long life already, to live forever. On 4 August 2000, the whole country marked her one-hundredth birthday, and accompanied by her grandson Prince Charles, she stood to greet the crowds and official delegations which had gathered. No one imagined that the end of her life was approaching.

But in early 2002 the elderly Queen Mother caught a cold and became stricken with a persistent cough. Elizabeth might have overcome this illness, as she had overcome illnesses more serious than this in the past. However, the untimely death of her younger daughter Margaret, had left the elderly woman in a weakened state, and only a few weeks passed before she herself passed away.

It came to pass on 30 March 2002, at 3:15 in the afternoon, Greenwich Mean Time, at her Royal Lodge home, that the elderly woman died in her sleep, her hand in the hand of her daughter Elizabeth II, and just four months shy of her one hundred and second birthday. Two and a half hours later Buckingham Palace announced the sad news and it was immediately taken up by the media worldwide. When the nation saw the newspapers on the same day, it was deeply shaken. The death of this royal dominated the news entirely. As one publisher noted, it is hard to imagine the death of a one hundred and one-year-old lady causing such emotion and commentary in any other country.

The British people looked back on all the years the Queen Mother had been with them, for so many years they felt as if Elizabeth would never meet a natural human end. Now her death made Britain remember that nothing on earth lasts forever.

The press showed a remarkable unanimity. The Queen Mother was praised and called the pillar of the Windsor family. Her role in supporting Britain's fighting spirit during World War II was recalled, and she was mourned as the last living witness to a departed era.

Crowds of people came to say their farewell to their beloved Queen Mother. On 9 April 2002 at 11:15, local time, the *grande dame*'s funeral ceremony began. Her coffin, clad in the flag of the United Kingdom, was carried out of The Palace of Westminster and placed on a carriage. Upon the one hundred and first toll of a bell, which marked the number of years the deceased had lived, the procession set off towards Westminster Abbey.

The funeral march was escorted by two hundred pipers and trumpeters (their lovely and sad Scottish melody was also featured in the opening of Mel Gibson's film *Braveheart*). The members of the royal family walked behind the coffin. Two Spitfire fighter planes (were they not the same which Lady MacRobert donated towards?) and a Lancaster bomber flew over the funeral procession. This modest air parade was a way of recognizing the Queen Mother's efforts during the war years.

As the documentation of this day shows us, in his eulogy, the Archbishop of Canterbury said, quoting from the book of Proverbs, "Many have done excellently, but you exceed them all." The ceremony ended with those present in Westminster Abbey singing "God Save the Queen".

The monarchess's body was buried at Windsor Castle, in the St George Chapel, next to her late husband King George VI. According to her will, the ashes of her younger daughter Princess Margaret, who had passed away two months earlier, were placed in the Queen Mother's grave.

Russia was represented at the funeral ceremony by its ambassador in London, Grigory Karasin. As for the Russian president at the time, Vladimir Putin sent Elizabeth II his condolences.

Thus, in accordance with the established rite, the elder Queen of Great Britain was laid to rest with the honours befitting a royal funeral, and not a state funeral, which is only held in the case of the reigning monarch's death. How do the two types differ? As Buckingham Palace explained to the media, the sole difference is that a royal funeral is paid for by the royal family, while the state covers the costs of a state funeral.

I must note that (according to publicly available information), the Queen's estate was subsequently distributed among her heirs, and it was valued at a total of one hundred million dollars, or around sixty million pounds sterling. The elder Elizabeth's primary heir was her grandson Prince Charles, but her great-grandsons William and Harry got four million each, and three million went to the reigning Queen Elizabeth II. The media claimed that the departed lady's bank account had a negative balance due to Her Majesty's fondness for betting on horse races. The sums accorded her by the Civil List, clearly did not cover this pastime. Even when she was still alive, as soon as it became widely known that this grandmother to the whole nation did not have enough funds, donations were sent in from across the nation to cover this royal deficit. All cheques were returned, with thanks, to their senders.

It is also noteworthy that besides the Civil List, Elizabeth II sent her mother two million pounds annually so that the latter could "maintain her aristocratic lifestyle". The salaries of the elder Elizabeth's staff were covered by her beloved grandson Prince Charles.

In Volgograd, the city of which the Queen Mother was now an honorary citizen, the flags were lowered outside all administrative buildings on 9 April 2002. At the Battle of Stalingrad Museum, a memorial service was held and the museum's director Boris Usik, gave the first speech. He explained how Her Majesty and her subjects had contributed to Stalingrad's defence and helped strengthen post-war ties. After the memorial service, attendees could view an exhibition dedicated to the Queen Mother and to the assistance which the British people had given to the defenders and residents of Stalingrad. These days, so sad for the whole world, served as the endpoint for my study of the life of Britain's elder queen.

Shortly thereafter, I was personally acquainted with Boris Usik. Allow me to refer to my diary from this period:

> Wonderfully, he agreed to sign my request. I came up with the text for it myself and sent it through to the secretary, and the document was returned to me on official paper with a signature

"M". With this paper in hand, it will no longer be embarrassing to meet the museum director.

Now the question was how to get to him. I was very worried that if I did not meet with the director personally, he would be indifferent to this paper and I would be met with refusal. But thank God, I managed to meet him. I just happened to bump into him at a reception and I handed him my request. He read it right there and then and then invited me to come see him in his office. Initially, Boris rather frightened me by asking the following question, loudly and completely unconcerned with the official document I had presented: why should he afford me an opportunity to research at the collection, when his own research staff could do it? But I managed to dodge any prickly issues here.

The director gave me some pushback, quizzed me about history. He was apparently hesitating whether to give me a yes or a no. He looked at the matter like this: if I could pass a history test, only then would I be permitted to do work at the collection. Unfortunately, I did not know the answer to his simple question about Shumilov, one of the soldiers who fought in the Battle of Stalingrad. To make up for that, I reminded him of the old joke, where it is one thing for a student to be able to name the number of Soviet deaths in World War II (twenty-seven million), and another thing to be able to identify them by name.

The museum director did not laugh, but clearly I had made inroads. He started to ask me questions more closely connected to my research: the date London was founded (I told him about William the Conqueror in 1066), as well as a question I already found elementary: where was the Queen Mother born. My answer: she was born to Lord and Lady Glamis in the family home, though there are contradictory accounts.

As a result, Mr Usik clapped my arm in a fatherly manner and signed my request.

Thus, I finally received permission to study the documents and historical items at the museum's British collection.

Her famous British humour

Many people, whose lives intersected with that of the Queen Mother, noted her endless reserves of good humour. Here are several stories about this which I have drawn from media reports.

Once, at dinner, when the Queen Mother was already nearing being a century old, a fish bone got stuck in her throat. Her home physician was unable to help her and they had to make an urgent visit to the hospital. When the fish bone was removed from Her Majesty's throat, the august lady quipped, "It's the salmon's revenge!"

Another episode from the life of the Queen Mother, which has figured in the press, is an anecdote that she herself liked to recount. The scene is an aged care facility where this elderly lady, a grandmother to the whole nation, has arrived on a charity visit. The visit was made with the usual fanfare: she is driven up in her beloved Rolls-Royce, she wears an elegant hat, veil, gloves. To make conversation, the august woman turns to an elderly gentleman and nods towards the rest of the elderly attendees:

"Do they know who I am?"

The old man answers, "Don't you worry! Just go to the reception desk and they'll tell you who you are!"

Another anecdote reported in the press has come from Elizabeth's own great-grandsons William and Harry. After the Queen Mother watched an episode of Sacha Baron Cohen's character Ali G, she learned to imitate his famous finger-snap and his catchphrase "Respect", with his distinctive diction. Later that day, after the family had gathered for lunch, the venerable old lady stood up from her chair, gave her thanks for the wonderful meal and, told her daughter the Queen "Respect", accompanied by the finger-snap. The others found it hilarious, Elizabeth II included. Why did the Queen Mother so love a good joke? It was because it could make interacting with her less tense. Everyone felt more at ease thanks to her sparkling sense of humour, and all the stiffness of the palace environment immediately evaporated.

She knew how to make her loved ones feel better with humour. For example, when her great-grandson William was leaving to study in Scotland, she noticed that he was feeling nervous, and with a smile she said, "Any good parties, invite me down." At once William felt more at ease.

Judging by these situations, the Queen Mother had not changed a bit since her youth, when her fans hung on her every word that came out of her mouth. Elizabeth was clearly destined to bring light, smiles and good spirits to the world around her. Was this not the secret to her charm?

As was later publicized, in 1966 the elder Elizabeth experienced one of the great health scares of her life. Doctors had discovered she had colon cancer. In December of the same year the Queen Mother was hospitalized for an operation to remove the malignant tumour. Though this surgical intervention was a success, for the following three months, all official events involving her were cancelled. At the same time, the press was told that the monarchess was merely undergoing treatment to remove a bowel obstruction. Only in Elizabeth's memoirs, published years after her death, did these days, so frightful for her, come to light.

I have often been asked what, in my opinion, was the secret to Elizabeth's long life. It has been claimed that it lies in her preference for non-alcoholic drinks. I am not inclined to agree with that, for the women among the British monarchy are generally known for their longevity, unlike their husbands. But the Queen Mother holds the record, having lived to the age of one hundred and one. The secret to living so long, I feel, mainly lies in her sense of humour, her positive attitude towards life and her love for overcoming hardships. She was fuelled by a certain lust for life, it kept her going on days both ordinary and grim. She never forgot the unspoken laws of royal honour: impeccable manners, a vivacious smile, no emotional outbursts, and she drew energy from this.

According to those around her, the elder Elizabeth, though she remained utterly devoted to her husband all her life long, preferred the company of men. This is a natural trait of women who stand at the peak of power.

Epilogue:
The battle for the monarchy
(twenty-first century)

No person was ever honored for what he received. Honor has been the reward for what he gave.

Calvin Coolidge, President of the USA

In summing up my study of the life of Elizabeth, I can confidently state that the Queen Mother was not crowned in 1936 in vain. Her reign opened up a new era for the institution of the monarchy: royal authority with "a human face". As a model pupil of her mother-in-law Queen Mary, the smiling Elizabeth brought something new into the way royals behaved: a charm and an openness to engaging with the population. With the advent of Elizabeth as Queen, people stopped viewing the royal family as something infinitely distant and alien. Now, the monarchy had come closer to the people, people could rely on it in times of hardship and expect help in resolving various problems.

For a clear example, let us turn to how Elizabeth II acted during her state visit to Russia in 1994. I have already written above about the positive impact this visit had for the British side. But the Queen did not neglect her traditional occupation, that is, charitable endeavours. I shall mention only some of the actions that Her Majesty took. When the Queen delivered her remarks at Saint-Petersburg State University, she told the students that the best of them could continue their studies at British institutions thanks to a new royal scholarship for foreign students.

Moreover, to strengthen business ties between our two countries, Elizabeth II kindly allowed her yacht *Britannia*, in Saint-Petersburg's port, to be used for a Russian–British business event while she was away. The topic of the meeting that was held on there, was how to stimulate investment in the Russian economy.

It is important to note one more action that Elizabeth II took for ordinary Russians: Her Majesty invited children from a Vyborg orphanage to tea with her on her yacht. These unusual guests were elated, for clearly it is not every day that one can meet the Queen, and not just anyone is given the opportunity.

The list of good deeds by Britain's royal family could continue with the heir to the throne, Prince Charles. He feels a great sense of responsibility with regard to his duties as the future monarch and he has already distinguished himself as a major figure in global philanthropy. As I mentioned before, the Prince of Wales has founded a large number of charitable foundations. One of the most important of his projects is giving disadvantaged youth opportunities for further education. The Prince himself has stated, to great applause, that a person's talent and personal qualities are more important than his or her background or skin colour.

Of course, we should not idealize the royal corporation, and there have been moments when it was not in tune with the needs or expectations of its subjects. At such moments the British press, which serves as an accurate barometer of the royal family's reputation, has jumped to sharply criticize them.

The British monarchy still lives on, unlike in many other countries, because it has found a role for itself in benefiting those in need. Philanthropy is the royals' main line of work. Whatever those opposed to the monarchy may claim, as long as the British crown is still of use to its people, as long as it aids in solving problems that trouble Britain, it will continue to enjoy respect and authority. How sincere are the members of the royal family in carrying out this role? That is a matter for politicians. We, however, prefer to think that it is a person's actions that best represent him or her.

In the last few decades, the Achilles heel of the British monarchy has been the turbulent love lives of its younger members. When one studies these recent marriages and affairs, one notes a certain regularity. As we recall, the Queen Mother, in her youth, was simply Lady Elizabeth, the first non-royal in three hundred years to marry one of the monarch's sons. Before her, only a titled Princess, one who had been brought up since childhood in a palace environment, could expect such a thing. It had to be a young lady who not only knew the rules of the royal game, but also understood why they were the way they were, and aimed to strictly follow them.

The focus of my study here, the provincial young lady Elizabeth from Scotland, coped like no other could with the new obligations placed upon her as a member of the royal family. Moreover, some feel that it was Elizabeth who saved the British monarchy by bringing into it her charm and openness, while also upholding the highest moral standards. However, Elizabeth proved merely an exception to the rule, for the other brides or grooms drawn from among Britain's mere mortals could not grasp the intricacies of life as a member of the royal family, and their marriages with their royal spouses collapsed.

Examples of such failed marriages are Princess Margaret (younger sister of Elizabeth II) and her husband, the talented photographer and filmmaker Antony Armstrong-Jones; Prince Charles and Lady Diana Spenser; Princess Anne and Mark Phillips; and Prince Andrew and Sarah Ferguson.

So, what do these intricate rules of palace life consist of?

One secret is probably that the main task of royal-family members is to preserve the monarchy. This is only possible if their own authority in their subjects' eyes is maintained. It is taxpayers who support the monarchy by paying them a Civil List income. To live up to this, one has to be (or at least appear to be) nearly infallible. After all, the monarchy is meant to represent the spirit and greatness of the nation.

These nuances are apparently capable of distinguishing those who are princes and princesses by blood, and striking a balance between their human weaknesses and the demands placed upon members of the royal family. What demands are these? One especially crucial quality in a monarchy is keeping abreast of its subjects' attitudes and expectations. Besides an appropriate dress code (no vulgar outfits or miniskirts) and assisting the disadvantaged strata of society, it is an important and delicate task of royal-family members to maintain the prestige of family values as they are understood worldwide. That means being faithful to one's spouse, mutual respect in the marriage, as well as an ability to seek agreement and, when necessary for higher purposes, strike a compromise.

The most responsible members of the royal family do visit hundreds of charitable events (even if they are sometimes rather dull ones) each year, and they help the government in establishing partnerships with other countries. Not everyone, however, has managed to avoid feeding the press with news about their marital troubles, and thus maintaining a positive image for the monarchy.

The *nouveau riche* of the royal family, who suddenly found themselves living in a glass house, have often been unable to cope with the new conditions, where they not only have to subordinate their own personal needs and complexes, but also serve a higher goal, that is, to preserve the monarchy for their descendants. Again, Her Majesty Queen Elizabeth The Queen Mother has acted in an exceptional manner and left the monarchy in a stronger position.

Some British biographers of royal family members have claimed that the Queen Mother's life was not as rosy as people think. The elder Elizabeth had her own disappointments in life. But once she became part of the royal family, she immediately learned that in order to maintain the authority of herself and her circle, sometimes she would have to bear matters in silence.

I have often been asked as a researcher, the following question. The Queen Mother was widowed very early (at the age of fifty-one) and she went on living for the same number of years. Did she have any romances with other men in her remaining years? The answer is that Her Majesty probably did remain eternally faithful to her late husband the King. Testimony for Elizabeth's dedication to her late husband can be found in her official biography, written by William Shawcross, which describes the elderly Elizabeth's indignation when American President Jimmy Carter tried to kiss her on the lips; no one, she claimed, had kissed her on the lips since her husband's death.

In this book I have said little about the Queen Mother's second daughter, Princess Margaret. There is a reason for that. When I gathered information about the members of the royal family, I came to know Margaret's life, too. Some authors (Sarah Bradford, Viktor Popov) have written, in detail, about it, but their accounts are similar, in that the most prominent aspect of Princess Margaret's life was her rocky relationships with the men she loved, and not acting for the good of the institution of the monarchy. Consequently, this princess strikes me as an unimpressive figure, and therefore an uninteresting one.

How should the reader view my work? I am no historian, and I cannot claim that this is a book of perfect rigour. Just as a sports commentator offers his observations and insights on what is being shown on the screen, revealing the little nuances, my work here has aimed to inform audiences less familiar with these matters and help them discern patterns and trends. As I am sure you will agree, a sporting event becomes more understandable and therefore, more exciting with an expert's commentary. The work I offer here represents my research into my chosen topic, and my elucidating commentary as an author who has studied these issues for several years.

Today, many public figures seek to gain a leading position in politics and, lacking any other example to go on, they draw their strategy from politicians of a class above: the monarchs. Whatever is visible on the surface of their lives has been set out in the present book, and the most important aspects of the monarchy have been assembled. Whoever seeks to boost their impact on society and political influence, let them study the monarchy and dare to apply what they have learned.

Appendix:
Elizabeth Angela Margaret Bowes-Lyon
(A Biographical Sketch)

Elizabeth, Queen of the United Kingdom from the Windsor dynasty and Queen Mother, was born Lady Elizabeth Angela Margaret Bowes-Lyon (4 August 1900 – 30 March 2002). Honorary citizen of the heroic city of Volgograd (2000). Head of some three hundred and fifty organizations. President of the British Red Cross Society (1937–1952). Commander-in-chief of all armies, the Women's Auxiliary Territorial Service and the women of the Royal Navy. Rector of the University of London (1955–1980). Holder of numerous other titles and honours.

She was born in London, UK, but the place of her birth was registered as St Paul's Walden Bury, Hertfordshire. Daughter of Claude George Bowes-Lyon (1855–1944) and Cecilia Nina Bowes-Lyon (1862–1938), the Lord and Lady of Glamis, named in 1904 the 14th Earl and Countess of Strathmore and Kinghorne.

Elizabeth was schooled at home. World War I broke out when she was fourteen years old. Her elder brothers left for the front. One, Fergus, was killed at the Battle of Loos (1915). Their family home, Glamis Castle, Scotland, was made a hospital for fifteen hundred wounded servicemen, and young Elizabeth assisted the adults in caring for them.

After her marriage to the Prince of York in 1923, Elizabeth became Duchess of York. On 21 April 1926, her first daughter was born, now Elizabeth II, Queen of the United Kingdom since 1952. A second daughter was Princess Margaret (1930–2002). After Edward VIII abdicated in 1936, the Duke and Duchess of York were crowned King George VI and Queen Elizabeth.

During World War II, Elizabeth and her family shared the same difficult fate as the entire nation. The royal residence, Buckingham Palace, was bombed nine times, but Elizabeth refused to be evacuated: "The Princesses would never leave without me and I couldn't leave without the King, and the King will never leave." These words have entered every British history textbook. Elizabeth visited areas most afflicted by the bombing, and also hospitals, factories, military bases and ordinary Londoners who had been left homeless. She worked day in and day out to morally support the nation and do good for it. The British called Elizabeth their "secret weapon", and Hitler believed her to be the most dangerous woman in Europe.

As president of the British Red Cross Society, Elizabeth lent support to the creation of the Aid to Russia Fund in autumn 1941. On 15 April 1945, the Fund's president Clementine Churchill, brought eight hundred and sixteen thousand and ninety-nine pounds sterling worth of hospital equipment to Stalingrad. In January 1943, through a Labourist Fund for aid to the USSR, one of Stalingrad's hospitals was outfitted. The British sent in 1943–1944, for Stalingrad's rebuilding of five portable power generators, four hundred thousand metres of electrical wiring and a phone switchboard for ten thousand numbers. The UK National Labour Organization sent Stalingrad a cheque for one hundred thousand pounds sterling to equip a city hospital. A joint committee for aid to the USSR, sent over two hundred thousand pounds sterling to build a Stalingrad hospital. Coventry workers raised twenty thousand pounds sterling to purchase medicines. In 1944, Stalingrad and Coventry became twin cities.

After Stalingraders' victory in the battle on the Volga in 1943, King George VI sent a gift of a sword of honour with the engraved text: "TO THE STEEL-HEARTED CITIZENS OF STALINGRAD, THE GIFT OF KING GEORGE THE SIXTH, IN TOKEN OF HOMAGE OF THE BRITISH PEOPLE".

In May 1999, in London, a memorial was raised, the work of Volgograd sculptor Sergei Shcherbakov, which was dedicated to the Soviet soldiers and civilians who died in World War II.

The title of honorary citizen of Stalingrad was awarded to Queen Mother Elizabeth by a resolution of the city's Council of People's Deputies in April 2000, for her distinguished services in arranging aid to Stalingrad from the British people during World War II and in developing friendly ties with Russia.

Bibliography

Antony Holden, *The Queen Mother: A Ninetieth Birthday Tribute* (London: Sphere, 1990).

Bertrand Meyer-Stabley, *Buckingham palace au temps d'Elisabeth II* (Paris: Hachette, 2007).

Boris Abalikhin, "Dar britanskikh narodov", *Otchij kray*, 1994, No. 1, pp. 209-213.

Britanskiy soyuznik, 5 December 1943, No. 49, p. 8.

Britanskiy soyuznik, 7 November 1942, No. 13, p. 7.

Carolly Erickson, *Lilibet: An Intimate Portrait of Queen Elizabeth II* (St. Martin's Press, 2005).

Clementine Churchill, *My Visit to Russia* (Hutchinson & Co., [1945]).

Dmitry Belov, "Solidarnost' britanskoy obshchestvennosti s grazhdanami Stalingrada v gody Velikoy otechestvennoy voyny", *Strezhen'*, Vol. 3. (Volgograd, 2003), pp. 67-72.

Edward Radzinsky, *Stalin* (Moscow, 2011).

Emil Ludwig, *Sud'ba korolya Eduarda* (Moscow, 2007).

Entsiklopediya Velikoy Otechestvennoy voyny 1941–1945 (Moscow, 1985).

G. S. Ostapenko, *Britanskaya monarkhiya ot korolevy Viktorii do Elizavety II* (Nauka, 2006).

Galina Mitrofanova, *Podarki iz Anglii kak simvol priznaniya geroicheskogo Stalingrada* (Volgograd, 1999).

Grania Forbes, *Elizabeth the Queen Mother: 1900–2002* (London: Pavilion, 2002).

Ingrid Seward, *The Last Great Edwardian Lady* (London: Century, 2002).

Ivan Maisky, *The Maisky Diaries: Red Ambassador to the Court of St James's, 1932–1943*, ed. by Gabriel Gorodetsky (New Haven: Yale University Press, 2015).

Ivan Maysky, *Vospominaniya sovetskogo diplomata* (Moscow: Mezhdunarodnye otnosheniya, 1987).

John Steinbeck, *A Russian Journal* (New York: Viking Press, 1948).

Lytton Strachey, *Queen Victoria* (1921).

M. A. Vodolagin, *Ocherki istorii Volgograda* (Moscow: Nauka, 1986).

Muzey gigieny i istorii zdravookhraneniya g. Volgograda. Inv. No. 1540.

Oleg Sakun, *Diplomaticheskoye remeslo* (Moscow, 2007).

Oleg Troyanovsky, *Iz kogorty vydayushchikhsya diplomatov* (Moscow, 2010).

P. M. H. Bell, *Twelve Turning Points of the Second World War* (New Haven: Yale University Press, 2011).

Sarah Bradford, *Elizabeth: A Biography of Britain's Queen* (New York: Farar, Straus and Giroux, 1996).

Stalingradskaya pravda. 8 April 1945.

Stalingraskaya pravda. 8 December 1943, No. 235 (4665).

The City We Loved: Coventry (W. H. Smith, 1948).

The Times, 7 December 1943.

V dni velikogo srazheniya: sbornik dokumentov i materialov o Stalingradskoy bitve (Stalingrad: Stalingradskoe knizhnoe izdatel'stvo, 1958).

V. I. Popov, *Sovetnik korolevy – superagent Kremlya* (Moscow: Mezhdunarodnye otnosheniya, 2005).

V. I. Popov, *Zhizhn' v Bukingemskom dvortse* (Moscow: Mezhdunarodnye otnosheniya, 1993).

V. M. Berezhkov, *Stranitsy diplomaticheskoy istorii* (Moscow: Mezhdunarodnye otnosheniya, 1987).

V. Sokolov and P. Stegny, *Mosty i baryery. Grazhdanskaya voyna i voennaya interventsiya v SSSR* (Moscow, 1987).

Vasily Zaytsev, *Thoughts of a Sniper*, trans. by David Givens, Peter Kornakov and Konstantin Kornakov, ed. by Neil Okrent (Los Angeles: 2826 Press, 2003).

Viktor Israelyan, *Diplomatiya – moya zhizn'* (MBA, 2006).

Viktor Popov, *Sovremennaya diplomatiya* (Moscow, 2003).

Vitaly Vul'f, *Zhenskoe litso Zapada* (Yauza, 2006).

Walter Schellenberg, *The Schellenberg Memoirs*, trans. by Louis Hagen (New York: André Deutsch, 1956).

William Shawcross, *Queen Elizabeth: The Queen Mother: The Official Biography* (Pan Macmillan, 2009).

Winston Churchill, *The Second World War. Vol. 3: The Grand Alliance* (Boston: Houghton Mifflin, 1950).

Yu. P. Tumanov, *Stalingrad – Coventry* (Stalingrad: Stalingradskoe knizhnoe izdatel'stvo, 1958).

Yury Dubinin, *Masterstvo peregovorov* (Moscow, 2009).

Yury Kashlev, *Diplomaticheskaya akademiya MID Rossii: istoria i sovremennost'* (Moscow, 2004).

The Queen Mother: Her Reign in Colour (Momentum, 2002) [on DVD].

PHOTOS AND DOCUMENTS
COURTESY OF NATALIA KULISHENKO
AND THE BATTLE
OF STALINGRAD MUSEUM

Official portrait of Queen Mother Elizabeth at the age of ninety, a gift to the city of Volgograd. Held in the Battle of Stalingrad Museum.

The Queen Mother, Ambassador Yury Fokin and his wife in St Paul's Cathedral, London, 31 October 1997.

Ambassador Yury Fokin and Vladimir Molchanov present the Queen Mother with the Queen statuette, 1999.

Ambassador Yury Fokin greets the Queen Mother on her birthday, Clarence House, London, 1999.

Reception to honour Arctic Convoy veterans at the Russian embassy, London, 1997.

Auto racers Prince Michael of Kent and Ambassador Yury Fokin.

Prince Michael of Kent and Ambassador Yury Fokin.

Ambassador Yury Fokin with the author, Moscow, 2010.

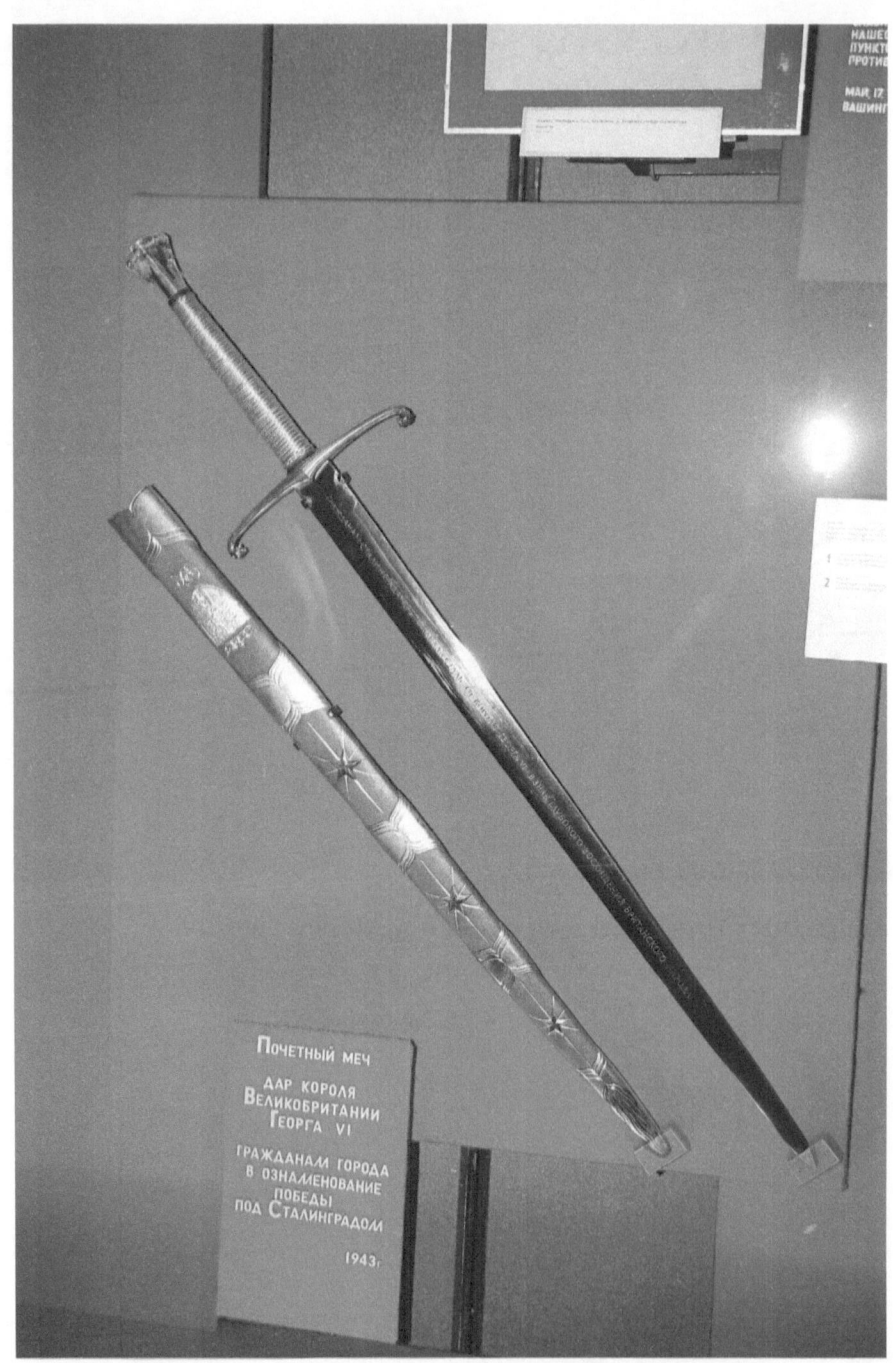

The sword of honour which King George VI gifted to Stalingrad in 1943.

Marshal Semyon Budenny shows the sword of George VI to the people of Stalingrad, 1944.

Princess Anne during a display of the sword, gifted by George VI, at the Battle of Stalingrad Museum, Volgograd, 1990.

Clementine Churchill during her visit to Stalingrad in April 1945.

The voice of the City

For female voices (S. S. A.)

Words by JACQUELINE MORRIS
(Pupil at Hengoed Girls' School, South Wales)

Music by ELIZABETH MACONCHY
(By consent of Hinrichsen Edition, Ltd.)

Staff and Tonic Solfa with piano accompaniment

NOTE: To make this song suitable for school choirs the Second Soprano and Alto parts have been kept as simple as possible throughout. Where possible, therefore, the more musically experienced singers should sing the First Soprano part. The passage up to bar 46 (✱) may be sung by a Solo voice.

Published by the   Copyright 1943
WORKERS' MUSIC ASSOCIATION
9, Great Newport Street,
London, W.C.2.

Printed in England

The title page of the song "The Voice of the City", published by Workers' Music Association in 1943.

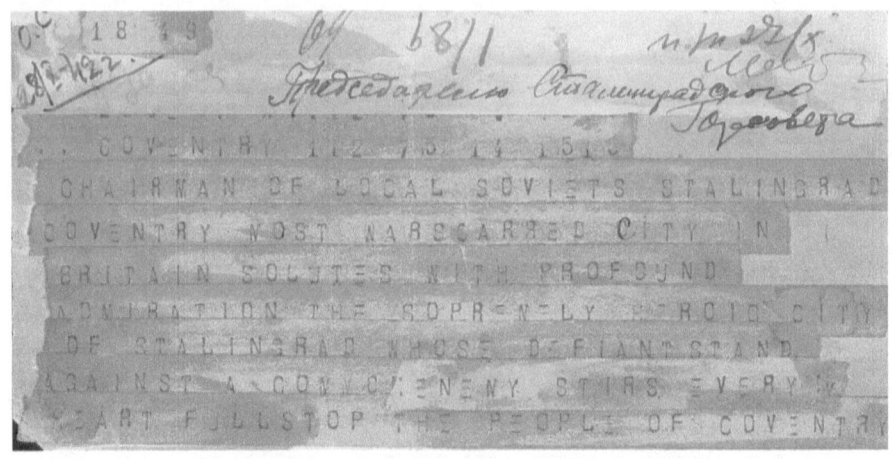

Alfred Robert Grindlay's telegram to Stalingrad, 16 September 1942.

Fundraising poster for the Aid to Russia Fund founded by Clementine Churchill, 1941.

Ticket to a Manchester dance on 17 September 1943, the earnings from which were marked for a Stalingrad hospital.

The royal spoon with the monogram of George VI, held in the museum as a symbol of British humanitarian assistance to Stalingrad.

President Vladimir Putin at the Soviet memorial during a state visit to the UK, London, 2003.

The Soviet memorial in London, created by sculptor Sergei Shcherbakov, 1999.

The identical memorial outside Volgograd (in Rossoshki), 2009.

Queen Elizabeth and King George VI tour the destruction wrought in Coventry by Nazi bombing, 1940.

Lady Godiva, the symbol of Coventry. Sculpture installed at St Mary's Guildhall.

Coventry Street in Volgograd (twin city to Coventry).

Lord Mayor of Coventry, Jack Harrison, and the author, Volgograd, 2010.

Lord Mayor Gary Crookes welcomes Russian delegates to Coventry and gifts are presented, 2013.

Lord Mayor Gary Crookes leads his Russian guests on a tour of Coventry, 2014.

LORD MAYOR'S PARLOUR
COUNCIL HOUSE
EARL STREET
COVENTRY
CV1 5RR

Telephone Number: 024 7683 3100
Fax Number: 024 7683 3078
E-mail: lord.mayor@coventry.gov.uk

April 2014

Natalia Kulishenko
37-2 Avenue Heroes of Stalingrad
Volgograd 400112
RUSSIA

Dear Natalia

May I commend you, on this year of the 70th anniversary of the twinning our two great cities, for all your contributions of work and efforts to deepen and strengthen the bi-lateral ties between Coventry and Volgograd. To this end your recent visits to my city have been expressly welcome.

I especially recognise your work as the author of the book: "To become a Queen. The Stalingrad Story of the British Queen," and the contribution it makes to Russian-British links. Her late Majesty, Queen Elizabeth, the Queen Mother was a great supporter of the people of Stalingrad, now Volgograd, and joined with the people of Coventry in offering encouragement to its people.

Yours sincerely

Councillor Gary Crookes
Lord Mayor of the City of Coventry

Lord Mayor Gary Crookes' letter of thanks to the author.

Drawing "The Queen of England" by Liza Kusmartseva, age 11, from *Drawings by Volgograd Schoolchildren Depicting Queen Elizabeth*, 2010.

Drawing "The Queen in the Garden" by Liza Kusmartseva, age 11, 2010.

Drawing "The Queen Having a Stroll" by Liza Rulyova, age 11, 2010.

Portrait of Princess Anne, a gift to the author, 2010.

At the Russian embassy in London. The author presents the first Russian-language edition to Deputy Prime Minister, Dmitry Rogozin, 2013.

13 Kensington Palace Gardens. Keepsake photo with Russian ambassador to the UK, Alexander Yakovenko, at his residence, London, 2013.

Natalia Kulishenko in the orangerie of the Russian embassy in London, 2013.

With Russian Foreign Minister, Sergei Lavrov, after a ceremony presenting him with the second Russian-language edition of the book, 2018.

МИНИСТР
ИНОСТРАННЫХ ДЕЛ
РОССИЙСКОЙ ФЕДЕРАЦИИ

«06» мая 2013г. № 2287/зв

Н.А. КУЛИШЕНКО

Уважаемая Наталия Алексеевна,

Благодарю Вас за теплое поздравление и добрые пожелания.

Признателен также за возможность ознакомиться с Вашей книгой о жизни и деятельности королевы Елизаветы. Ваша работа позволяет расширить знания о династии Виндзоров, содержит интересные факты из истории отношений между Россией и Великобританией, прежде всего в период Второй мировой войны.

Уверен, что Ваш труд будет интересен не только историкам и специалистам-международникам, но и всем, кто занимается проблемами внешней политики и дипломатии.

Желаю Вам новых творческих успехов и всего самого доброго.

Искренне,

С. ЛАВРОВ

Letter from Russian Foreign Minister, Sergei Lavrov, to the author after the publication of the first Russian-language edition, 2013.

Mikhail Bulgakov: The Life and Times
by Marietta Chudakova

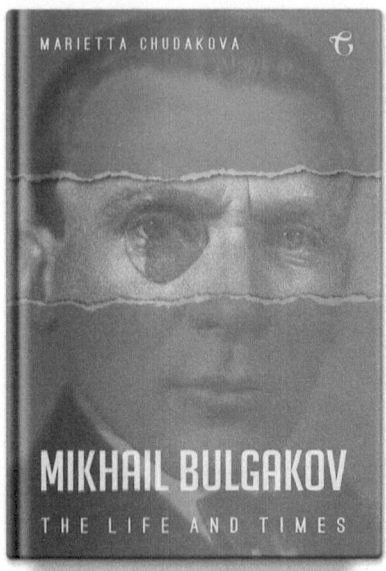

Marietta Chudakova's biography of Bulgakov was first published in 1988 and remains the most authoritative and comprehensive study of the writer's life ever produced. It has received acclaim for the journalistic style in which it is written: the author draws on unpublished manuscripts and early drafts of Bulgakov's novels to bring the writer to life. She also explores archive documents and memoirs written by some of Bulgakov's contemporaries so as to construct a comprehensive and nuanced portrait of the writer and his life and times. The scholar casts light on Bulgakov's life with an unrivalled eye for detail and a huge amount of affection for the writer and his works.

Mikhail Bulgakov: The Life and Times will be of particular interest to international researchers studying Mikhail Bulgakov's life and works, and is recommended to a broader audience worldwide.

Buy it > www.glagoslav.com

The Nuremberg Trials
by Alexander Zvyagintsev

Postwar Nuremberg is set to host a historically unprecedented trial of the leaders of the defeated Third Reich. The whole world is awaiting a just verdict, but it is here where Soviet counterintelligence must wage a secret war against forces that seek to prevent that from happening at any cost. Nuremberg, having been nearly wiped from the face of the earth during the harsh fighting, becomes an arena for ruthless struggles in both hidden and overt operations. Nazis are still operating underground, spies weave their intrigues, politicians and diplomats make bargains, and movie stars dazzle the public. The enormous efforts led by the USSR's chief prosecutor Roman Rudenko to expose the Nazi atrocities are threatened.

The Nuremberg Trials is based upon real facts that were hitherto unknown and details that the author, who spent many years studying the trials, learned from participants and witnesses.

Buy it > www.glagoslav.com

The Flying Dutchman
by Anatoly Kudryavitsky

Some time in the 1970s, Konstantin Alpheyev, a well-known Russian musicologist, finds himself in trouble with the KGB, the Russian secret police, after the death of his girlfriend, for which one of their officers may have been responsible. He has to flee from the city and to go into hiding. He rents an old house located on the bank of a big Russian river, and lives there like a recluse observing nature and working on his new book about Wagner. The house, a part of an old barge, undergoes strange metamorphoses rebuilding itself as a medieval schooner, and Alpheyev begins to identify himself with the Flying Dutchman. Meanwhile, the police locate his new whereabouts and put him under surveillance. A chain of strange events in the nearby village makes the police officer contact the KGB, and the latter figure out who the new tenant of the old house actually is.

Buy it > www.glagoslav.com

I Want a Baby and Other Plays
by Sergei Tretyakov

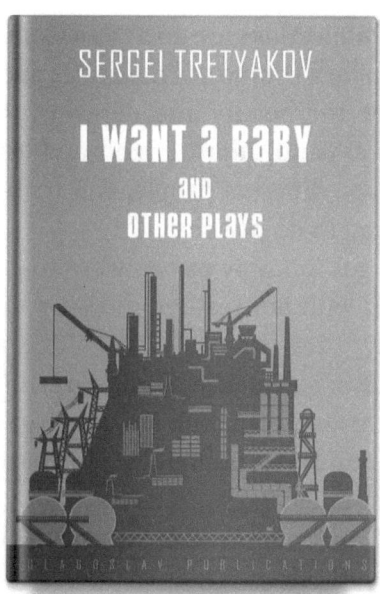

When Sergei Tretyakov's ground-breaking play, *I Want a Baby*, was banned by Stalin's censor in 1927, it was a signal that the radical and innovative theatre of the early Soviet years was to be brought to an end. A glittering, unblinking exploration of the realities of post-revolutionary Soviet life, *I Want a Baby* marks a high point in modernist experimental drama.

Tretyakov's plays are notable for their formal originality and their revolutionary content. *The World Upside Down*, which was staged by Vsevolod Meyerhold in 1923, concerns a failed agrarian revolution. *A Wise Man*, originally directed by the great film director and Tretyakov's friend, Sergei Eisenstein, is a clown show set in the Paris of the émigré White Russians. *Are You Listening, Moscow?!* and *Gas Masks* are 'agit-melodramas', fierce, fast-moving and edgy...

Buy it > www.glagoslav.com

Dear Reader,

Thank you for purchasing this book.

We at Glagoslav Publications are glad to welcome you, and hope that you find our books to be a source of knowledge and inspiration.

We want to show the beauty and depth of the Slavic region to everyone looking to expand their horizon and learn something new about different cultures, different people, and we believe that with this book we have managed to do just that.

Now that you've got to know us, we want to get to know you. We value communication with our readers and want to hear from you! We offer several options:

– Join our Book Club on Goodreads, Library Thing and Shelfari, and receive special offers and information about our giveaways;

– Share your opinion about our books on Amazon, Barnes & Noble, Waterstones and other bookstores;

– Join us on Facebook and Twitter for updates on our publications and news about our authors;

– Visit our site www.glagoslav.com to check out our Catalogue and subscribe to our Newsletter.

Glagoslav Publications is getting ready to release a new collection and planning some interesting surprises — stay with us to find out!

Glagoslav Publications
Email: contact@glagoslav.com

Glagoslav Publications Catalogue

- *The Time of Women* by Elena Chizhova
- *Andrei Tarkovsky: The Collector of Dreams* by Layla Alexander-Garrett
- *Andrei Tarkovsky - A Life on the Cross* by Lyudmila Boyadzhieva
- *Sin* by Zakhar Prilepin
- *Hardly Ever Otherwise* by Maria Matios
- *Khatyn* by Ales Adamovich
- *The Lost Button* by Irene Rozdobudko
- *Christened with Crosses* by Eduard Kochergin
- *The Vital Needs of the Dead* by Igor Sakhnovsky
- *The Sarabande of Sara's Band* by Larysa Denysenko
- *A Poet and Bin Laden* by Hamid Ismailov
- *Watching The Russians (Dutch Edition)* by Maria Konyukova
- *Kobzar* by Taras Shevchenko
- *The Stone Bridge* by Alexander Terekhov
- *Moryak* by Lee Mandel
- *King Stakh's Wild Hunt* by Uladzimir Karatkevich
- *The Hawks of Peace* by Dmitry Rogozin
- *Harlequin's Costume* by Leonid Yuzefovich
- *Depeche Mode* by Serhii Zhadan
- *The Grand Slam and other stories (Dutch Edition)* by Leonid Andreev
- *METRO 2033 (Dutch Edition)* by Dmitry Glukhovsky
- *METRO 2034 (Dutch Edition)* by Dmitry Glukhovsky
- *A Russian Story* by Eugenia Kononenko
- *Herstories, An Anthology of New Ukrainian Women Prose Writers*
- *The Battle of the Sexes Russian Style* by Nadezhda Ptushkina
- *A Book Without Photographs* by Sergey Shargunov
- *Down Among The Fishes* by Natalka Babina
- *disUNITY* by Anatoly Kudryavitsky
- *Sankya* by Zakhar Prilepin
- *Wolf Messing* by Tatiana Lungin
- *Good Stalin* by Victor Erofeyev
- *Solar Plexus* by Rustam Ibragimbekov

- *Don't Call me a Victim!* by Dina Yafasova
- *Poetin (Dutch Edition)* by Chris Hutchins and Alexander Korobko
- *A History of Belarus* by Lubov Bazan
- *Children's Fashion of the Russian Empire* by Alexander Vasiliev
- *Empire of Corruption - The Russian National Pastime* by Vladimir Soloviev
- *Heroes of the 90s: People and Money. The Modern History of Russian Capitalism*
- *Fifty Highlights from the Russian Literature (Dutch Edition)* by Maarten Tengbergen
- *Bajesvolk (Dutch Edition)* by Mikhail Khodorkovsky
- *Tsarina Alexandra's Diary (Dutch Edition)*
- *Myths about Russia* by Vladimir Medinskiy
- *Boris Yeltsin: The Decade that Shook the World* by Boris Minaev
- *A Man Of Change: A study of the political life of Boris Yeltsin*
- *Sberbank: The Rebirth of Russia's Financial Giant* by Evgeny Karasyuk
- *To Get Ukraine* by Oleksandr Shyshko
- *Asystole* by Oleg Pavlov
- *Gnedich* by Maria Rybakova
- *Marina Tsvetaeva: The Essential Poetry*
- *Multiple Personalities* by Tatyana Shcherbina
- *The Investigator* by Margarita Khemlin
- *The Exile* by Zinaida Tulub
- *Leo Tolstoy: Flight from paradise* by Pavel Basinsky
- *Moscow in the 1930* by Natalia Gromova
- *Laurus (Dutch edition)* by Evgenij Vodolazkin
- *Prisoner* by Anna Nemzer
- *The Crime of Chernobyl: The Nuclear Goulag* by Wladimir Tchertkoff
- *Alpine Ballad* by Vasil Bykau
- *The Complete Correspondence of Hryhory Skovoroda*
- *The Tale of Aypi* by Ak Welsapar
- *Selected Poems* by Lydia Grigorieva
- *The Fantastic Worlds of Yuri Vynnychuk*

- *The Garden of Divine Songs and Collected Poetry of Hryhory Skovoroda*
- *Adventures in the Slavic Kitchen: A Book of Essays with Recipes*
- *Seven Signs of the Lion by Michael M. Naydan*
- *Forefathers' Eve by Adam Mickiewicz*
- *One-Two by Igor Eliseev*
- *Girls, be Good by Bojan Babić*
- *Time of the Octopus by Anatoly Kucherena*
- *The Grand Harmony by Bohdan Ihor Antonych*
- *The Selected Lyric Poetry Of Maksym Rylsky*
- *The Shining Light by Galymkair Mutanov*
- *The Frontier: 28 Contemporary Ukrainian Poets - An Anthology*
- *Acropolis: The Wawel Plays by Stanisław Wyspiański*
- *Contours of the City by Attyla Mohylny*
- *Conversations Before Silence: The Selected Poetry of Oles Ilchenko*
- *The Secret History of my Sojourn in Russia by Jaroslav Hašek*
- *Mirror Sand: An Anthology of Russian Short Poems*
- *Maybe We're Leaving by Jan Balaban*
- *Death of the Snake Catcher by Ak Welsapar*
- *A Brown Man in Russia by Vijay Menon*
- *Hard Times by Ostap Vyshnia*
- *The Flying Dutchman by Anatoly Kudryavitsky*
- *Nikolai Gumilev's Africa by Nikolai Gumilev*
- *Combustions by Srđan Srdić*
- *The Sonnets by Adam Mickiewicz*
- *Dramatic Works by Zygmunt Krasiński*
- *Four Plays by Juliusz Słowacki*
- *Little Zinnobers by Elena Chizhova*
- *We Are Building Capitalism! Moscow in Transition 1992-1997*
- *The Nuremberg Trials by Alexander Zvyagintsev*
- *The Hemingway Game by Evgeni Grishkovets*
- *A Flame Out at Sea by Dmitry Novikov*
- *Jesus' Cat by Grig*
- *Want a Baby and Other Plays by Sergei Tretyakov*
- *I Mikhail Bulgakov: The Life and Times by Marietta Chudakova*
- *Leonardo's Handwriting by Dina Rubina*

- *A Burglar of the Better Sort* by Tytus Czyżewski
- *The Mouseiad and other Mock Epics* by Ignacy Krasicki
- *Ravens before Noah* by Susanna Harutyunyan
- Duel by Borys Antonenko-Davydovych
- *An English Queen and Stalingrad* by Natalia Kulishenko
- *Point Zero* by Narek Malian
- *Absolute Zero* by Artem Chekh
- *Olanda* by Rafał Wojasiński
- *Robinsons* by Aram Pachyan
- *The Monastery* by Zakhar Prilepin
- *The Selected Poetry of Bohdan Rubchak: Songs of Love, Songs of Death, Songs of the Moon*
- *Everyday Stories* by Mima Mihajlović
- *Mebet* by Alexander Grigorenko
- *The Orchestra* by Vladimir Gonik
- *Slavdom* by Ľudovít Štúr
- *De Zwarte Kip* by Antoni Pogorelski (Dutch Edition)
- *The Revolt of the Animals* by Wladyslaw Reymont
- *The Village Teacher and Other Stories* by Theodore Odrach
- *Sergei Tretyakov: A Revolutionary Writer in Stalin's Russia* by Robert Leach

More coming soon...

www.ingramcontent.com/pod-product-compliance
Lightning Source LLC
Chambersburg PA
CBHW021433080526
44588CB00009B/513